SAGE was founded in 1965 by Sara Miller McCune to support the dissemination of usable knowledge by publishing innovative and high-quality research and teaching content. Today, we publish over 900 journals, including those of more than 400 learned societies, more than 800 new books per year, and a growing range of library products including archives, data, case studies, reports, and video. SAGE remains majority-owned by our founder, and after Sara's lifetime will become owned by a charitable trust that secures our continued independence.

Los Angeles | London | New Delhi | Singapore | Washington DC | Melbourne

ADVANCE PRAISE

While looking at the 'first-time managers' for multi-locational team handling, it is important to understand the background and context of the team, including the operating managers and the others in the group. This is aptly captured in the book.

Mukund Rajan, *Chairman, ECube Investment Advisors*

The book deals with a very bold topic in simple terms. Having personally gone through various roles in corporate corridors of an individual contributor, first-time manager and skip over a long career, I could relate with what Rishi brings out of organizational structures and roles. The culture, mindset, decision-making, struggles of letting go and myth of wisdom sitting at the top are dealt with, in simple examples, for one to relate and drive a change. For those who are evolving through the roles up, it becomes a fine reference handbook and helps develop the skill and the will to deal and respond to organizational dynamics. A delightful read coming from a seasoned thinker, practitioner, trainer and coach. Thanks, Rishi. I have made important notes in my diary.

Rajesh Padmanabhan, *CEO, Talavvy, a Senior Business Transformational Leader*

Challenges of leading teams skip management and executive isolation are the ones that play out in every organization, only the scale may vary. Essential attributes of a successful company are its ability to prepare individual contributors to be effective managers and guide chief experience officers to wade off executive isolation. I am fortunate to have been part of large global organizations such as Tatas, Ericsson, Sony Mobile and Nokia to name a few and the journey is ongoing.

I, like many others, have aspired to develop managers with futuristic leadership skills. During my assignment as managing director of Sony Ericsson India/Sony Mobile India, Rishi reported to me as the vice-president for institutional business. His knack for business management and client relationships always brought gains to the organization. It's a pleasure to know of his continuous drive to share his wealth of experience with new-age managers and academia, who will highly benefit from these insights. As his well-wisher and as a professional, I will be looking forward to his book that touches upon lesser spoken but important elements which can make or break great companies.

P. Balaji, *Chief Regulatory and Corporate Affairs Officer, Vodafone Idea Limited, Former Managing Director, Nokia India and Sony Mobile Communications India*

When soldiers are becoming leaders in a frontline role, you are used to an upward management. Suddenly in a managerial role, you have both upward and downward management, and handling both is very sensitive and needs finesse. Read more about this in the book.

Anil Nair, *Managing Director, Country Digital Acceleration, Cisco APJC*

Having grown up the ranks and now heading Qualcomm as vice-president and president, India and SAARC, I have personally experienced the nuances of managing multi-location teams. Creating the right working culture in the organization is the most important aspect of high levels of team performance.

The morale of a team depends a lot on the attitude and the tone that leaders exhibit while talking to them, including skip managers. I have known Rishi for a decade, starting as a partner-customer and later as colleagues till Rishi chartered his course to be an author. His book deals with extremely pertinent matters of managing multicultural teams, contexts of global offices, skip management and how not to feel lonely at the top. I wish him luck and hope to get my hands on the book soon.

Rajen Vagadia, *Vice-president and President, Qualcomm India and SAARC*

Managers may try to keep their bosses isolated from the teams due to the deep-rooted fear that the team members may complain about the managers' management style or ineffectiveness. Read on how to deal with executive isolation and skip management.

Lloyd Mathias, *Pan-Asia Business Leader*

Managing LARGE TEAMS

Overcoming Skip-Level Frictions and Executive Isolation

Rishi Kapal

Los Angeles | London | New Delhi
Singapore | Washington DC | Melbourne

Copyright © Rishi Kapal, 2021

All rights reserved. No part of this book may be reproduced or utilized in any form or by any means, electronic or mechanical, including photocopying, recording or by any information storage or retrieval system, without permission in writing from the publisher.

First published in 2021 by

SAGE Publications India Pvt. Ltd
B1/I-1 Mohan Cooperative Industrial Area
Mathura Road, New Delhi 110 044, India
www.sagepub.in

SAGE Publications Inc
2455 Teller Road
Thousand Oaks, California 91320, USA

SAGE Publications Ltd
1 Oliver's Yard, 55 City Road
London EC1Y 1SP, United Kingdom

SAGE Publications Asia-Pacific Pte Ltd
18 Cross Street #10-10/11/12
China Square Central
Singapore 048423

Published by Vivek Mehra for SAGE Publications India Pvt. Ltd. Typeset in 11.5/14.5 pt Bembo by Fidus Design Pvt. Ltd, Chandigarh.

Library of Congress Control Number: 2020949545

ISBN: 978-93-5388-672-1 (PB)

SAGE Team: Namarita Kathait, Shruti Gupta, Aanchal Jain and Rajinder Kaur

To the skip managers and supervisors who contributed to my learning and development.

Thank you for choosing a SAGE product!
If you have any comment, observation or feedback,
I would like to personally hear from you.

Please write to me at **contactceo@sagepub.in**

Vivek Mehra, Managing Director and CEO, SAGE India.

Bulk Sales
SAGE India offers special discounts
for purchase of books in bulk.
We also make available special imprints
and excerpts from our books on demand.

For orders and enquiries, write to us at

Marketing Department
SAGE Publications India Pvt Ltd
B1/I-1, Mohan Cooperative Industrial Area
Mathura Road, Post Bag 7
New Delhi 110044, India

E-mail us at **marketing@sagepub.in**

Subscribe to our mailing list
Write to **marketing@sagepub.in**

This book is also available as an e-book.

Foreword by T. N. Hari ix
Preface xi
Acknowledgements xiii

Ch 1: Experiences as a First-Time Manager 1
Ch 2: Decoding Effective Business Structures and Hierarchies 31
Ch 3: Dynamics between Managerial Levels: The Dos and Don'ts! 67
Ch 4: Truth About Managing Large Teams 93
Ch 5: Breaking through Executive Isolation 123
Ch 6: Trading Relationships with Results: Attachment Inhibiting Detachment 149
Ch 7: Building Trust: Effective Motivation 171
Ch 8: Becoming a Better Manager 191

About the Author 213

People make organizations. As individuals progress through their career, they need to make some key transitions. The first transition is often about moving from being an individual contributor to managing a team. The next transition is about leading a bunch of individuals who manage teams. Managers who manage people who in turn manage teams are often referred to as skip-level managers in common parlance. Skip-level managing is not the same as managing a team directly and is actually a different ball game altogether. A few of the individuals make it to a CXO role. And here the individual is part of the executive management, the apex leadership team in the company. This calls for an altogether different order of leadership.

This book is about handling these transitions well. Every transition requires the individual concerned to learn a set of new skills and, at the same time, give up a few things that he/she was doing earlier. Giving up something that has been deeply engrained into your personality and identity is not easy and calls for as much effort as learning new skills. Each of these transitions also create some stress and, hence, it is helpful to have a coach or a mentor who can help with this process.

Just as individuals go through key transitions in their careers, organizations too go through phase changes as they evolve from being a start-up to a mature firm. The organization too needs to collectively master the ability to handle these phase changes. As the firm becomes multi-locational and global, the complexities increase exponentially, and the leadership skills need far more refinement and sophistication. Leading multicultural and virtual teams is in itself an art. Leading in a crisis is another competence altogether and in a rapidly changing environment, crises will always be lurking around the corner.

Rishi's book *Managing Large Teams* deals with the nuances of each of these transitions well. It is a good guide to help individuals navigate their way through their leadership journey.

I wish him luck.

T. N. Hari
Head HR, Bigbasket, and Strategic Advisor,
Fundamentum Partnership

PREFACE

It was a career of 21 years during which I embarked on a journey from being a customer engineer in 1993 to a CEO (interim MD and VP of Sony Mobile India) in 2013–2014. During the course of my two decades of corporate life, the experiences of becoming a first-time manager, learning the art to manage multi-locational and multicultural teams, embracing the nuances of skip management and eventually experiencing executive isolation were a part and parcel of the journey. Post my active corporate career, I started consulting mid/senior management professionals on career management and identified unique threads of challenges that they faced. This book is an amalgamation of my journey and the experiences of coaching 250 odd professionals in the last 6 years.

The motivation and inspiration to write this book were based on the urge to share my organization development experiences coupled with interviews of global industry leaders. The process of writing this book led me to research and understand about various syndromes at work, namely the special snowflake and yes man syndromes. It was a challenging process over the last one year to understand the nuances of managing large teams under the context of skip management and executive isolation. This book needed a granular and practical view of organization development not just through my eyes.

The urge to offer compelling and practice-oriented work took me to industry leaders for their experiences and wisdom to become a part of the book. Such amazing global leaders including Dr Mukund Rajan, Mr Anil Nair, Mr T. N. Hari, Mr P. Balaji,

Mr Lloyd Mathias, Mr Rajesh Padmanabhan, Mr Rajen Vagadia and my esteemed community members of the Stanford LEAD alumni programme across the world agreed to help me with their experiences, which are adequately mentioned in the book.

Happy reading to build great careers and organizations.

ACKNOWLEDGEMENTS

In life you come across people who share your purpose, cause and vision. I take this opportunity to thank them for sharing their experiences which enriched this book and kept me motivated to write.

Dr Mukund Rajan is the Chairman of ECube Investment Advisors Private Limited. Prior to ECube, Dr Rajan served for 23 years with the Tata Group, where he held a number of senior executive positions. It is my privilege to have known him for the last couple of years, and I met him first when he was heading Tata Teleservices (Maharashtra) Limited as a managing director.

Mr Anil Nair is the Managing Director, Country Digital Acceleration at Cisco APJC. Prior to that he held CEO and CXO roles at AGC Networks, Securitas and Aegis to name a few. It was a blessing for me to have worked at Tata Telecom/ Avaya under Anil's leadership.

Mr Lloyd Mathias, a pan-Asia business leader, marketer and strategist with intimate knowledge of the region and a proven track record of creating compelling visons and driving business performance across the consumer, telecom and technology domains. Lloyd has led HP, Motorola, Tata and Pepsi. I had the honour to know Lloyd since my days at Qualcomm and his president role at Tata Teleservices.

Mr T. N. Hari is a celebrated industry professional, currently the Head HR, Bigbasket, and Strategic Advisor, Fundamentum Partnership. He is extremely passionate about solving problems and building organizations for scale through clear and uncluttered thinking and relentless execution.

My heartfelt thanks to batchmates, alumni of Stanford LEAD programme and well-wishers in the professional network.

Saul Jaeger, MSESM
Police Captain at Mountain View Police Department, USA

Sachio Nishioka
Deloitte/Regional Ambassador for Stanford GSB Corporate Innovation for Asia

Massimo Mercuri
Co-founder at AlterContacts, Netherlands

Balaji Ramakrishnan
Information & Data Services at Adobe, India

Lisa Sabilia
Co-CEO at Youtopian, USA

Vijaya Vardhan Panthagani
EMEA Customer Support and Success Manager at Atlassian, India

Eklavya Upadhyay
Strategy, Innovation, Transformation Specialist, USA

Scott Butcher
Finance Dedicated Services at Google, USA

Anirvan Sen
Chief Executive Officer at Fifth Chrome, Netherlands

Geoffrey Lewis
TEDxSUU Speaker, Deputy Director SUU, USA

Marta Ferrer Garcia
Production, Babieka, Spain

Shankar Mallapur
Life and Career Coach, India

Juana-Catalina Rodriguez
Innovation, Strategy, Design Thinker at Thales, France

Ruchi Tandon
Director at SAP SuccessFactors, USA

EXPERIENCES AS A FIRST-TIME MANAGER

Managers are like babies; they scream every half an hour to wake up the people around them.

Becoming a manager is a step up in anyone's career. However, the initial days in the role set the groundwork for a person's future as a manager. In this chapter you can expect to read about the challenges faced by a first-time manager (FTM), real life experiences of FTMs and how to mitigate the challenges. Not everyone is successful in a managerial capacity since some people are better suited to being individual contributors for a long time. This book will answer the questions you have to help you decide whether being a manager is your cup of tea.

The quality of managers decides the fate of a company to a large extent. When people are elevated as managers, it's a reflection of their individual performance, a demonstration of their work ethics and evidence of their ability to lead from the front. However, elevating someone from an individual contributor to a manager doesn't always guarantee success.

Becoming a manager for the first time can be exciting as well as overwhelming. The journey from being an individual contributor to becoming a manager is not an easy transition; a successful transition requires a large skill set, including effective communication, ability to coach and motivate reportees and most importantly, a capacity to listen with intent. Every individual contributor, who gets an opportunity to become a manager, needs to develop such a skill-set—understanding the team, delegating, taking feedback—and essentially learning through trial and error in order to make the transition smoother and quicker.

Lesser explored than the transition from classrooms to the corporate desk, but equally relevant in one's career is the transition from an individual contributor to an FTM. Managing well is the beginning to being an effective leader; it is a role that advances from being an individual contributor (IC) to an FTM and ultimately a skip manager (the manager's manager). One can be promoted to an FTM in their current organization or by a vertical transition to a new company. For perspective, I will relate a real-life experience of becoming an FTM in a new organization, which also sets the stage for the interplay between FTMs and skip managers and how it starts to take shape early on.

It's quite often that FTMs find themselves elevated from among a group of people who were once peers. After such elevation, they have to manage and instruct the same group of people, keeping personal relationships, which may have developed over time, aside. Becoming a manager changes one's relationships with ex-peers and colleagues; absolute transparency in management is key in succeeding in such cases. If not balanced appropriately, the management starts to get clouded, with personal relationships driving managerial decisions from the forefront.

LEARNING TO MANAGE IS HARD

In the first month of taking charge, one of the foremost things the new managers realize is that the role is much more demanding than they expected. It can be a drain on the nerves as well as completely test one's patience. Most of the first-time managers are taken by surprise when they realize that the skills they acquired and developed to be successful individual contributors are very different from the ones they need in order to be effective managers. The FTMs realize that there is a striking gap between their existing abilities and the abilities required in order to succeed in their new position.

As individual contributors, their success or failure was dependent on personal skills and experiences. But as managers, their responsibilities include setting objectives, not just for themselves but for their team as well, and ensuring that the action-plan is executed as a group. Their experiences as individual performers do not prepare them to be successful managers.

Take the case of Amit, who was a stellar, best-performing sales executive I had. He had been in sales for six years and was being groomed to become a manager for customer management. He was an aggressive sales professional with an innovative streak. It took me only a year to recognize that Amit would make a good manager and I was ready to give him the opportunity when the time came. No one would have been surprised with his promotion to a manager since everyone respected his achievements and humility. I recall him telling me at times that there was simply too much on my plate and that he could make life better for me by taking up additional responsibility. Amit was saying all the right things at the right time. I had a week-long discussion with Amit about what was in store for him and he claimed to understand what it takes to be an effective manager. I also made sure he knew that I would continue to coach him, but only for the initial period. So came the day I promoted him to a manager and Amit's peers began reporting to him. I started to focus more on strategies, taking fortnightly review meetings and felt confident that Amit would be doing his part, handling the tactical decision-making. After six weeks into the role as a manager, Amit walked into my office. I noticed he had lost his usual smile and confidence.

I asked him to sit down and offered him some coffee. He said that it was harder than he imagined leading people he used to work with side by side and even more difficult to get his ideas implemented by them. However, he also understood that there was no security blanket and he had to face his responsibilities as there was no turning back.

Amit's reaction about being uncertain as a manager was a shock to him, but I knew it wasn't unusual. Ability to lead develops by experience; knowing how to manage cannot be taught, it is learnt by doing and not giving up. Becoming a manager for the first time is not a subject which has a set syllabus. However, it requires coaching from the level two managers; help may be voluntarily offered, or a new manager may ask for it, the way Amit came to me. While being a good manager cannot be taught in a classroom, the science and art behind effective management can be learnt through on-the-job experiences; new managers need to stretch beyond their comfort zone professionally and emotionally. One of the most important aspects of being a first-time manager is to ensure that the team doesn't think of them as a trial and error (T & E) guy. Amit, as an individual contributor seldom made mistakes. As such, it was new to him, and is generally new for every FTM, to handle the stress of owning the negative outcomes of his team's performance. During our chat, I made two offers to Amit: First, he can come and informally chat with me every alternate day to discuss how things are going. Second, I offered to take parallel charge of the team with him, since I was their skip manager. Living up to my expectations, Amit declined the second offer and agreed to the former. He started learning the tricks of being a manager gradually. By the time I was moving out of the organization to take on a new assignment, Amit had proven his worth to potentially be my successor. He was a great CXO in the making.

During an FTM's lifetime, they have much to learn as well as unlearn. Whatever made them successful in the early years of their careers, needs to improve ten-fold to allow their new and stronger professional identities to emerge. An FTM introspects about new thinking practices like investing in understanding people, being assertive, complimenting good work and practising effective communication, and figures out different ways of setting goals, agreeing to key performance indicators (KPI) with teams and measuring success: That is when one starts to derive satisfaction from the role. Many employees complain that a promotion to manager is painful. However, if they survive the tough years, they find that the fruits of their labour and pain are equally rewarding. Nonetheless, there are many professionals who go back to individual contributor roles and make the most out of it.

The FTMs generally ask themselves two questions: Would I like to be a manager; is it going to be enjoyable and will I be a good manager, good enough to rise through the ranks? There are no right or wrong answers to these questions, however, the FTMs continue to question themselves, every day.

Becoming a manager does not present a bleak picture, however, the fact is that most individual contributors find it unsettling to become a manager. This mostly happens because, in the beginning, they associate becoming a manager with prestige rather than increase in responsibilities.

Something that has been said since generations of management practices and organization behaviour is that more than leaving companies, people leave managers. However, organizations seldom realize that maybe the talent erosion and attrition is not due to the direct manager. It is often not realized that second- or third-level managers and proclaimed leaders (skip-level managers) have a major impact on morale, employee engagement, retention and attrition. Every Stanford LEAD alumni, whether CXOs, law enforcement specialists or entrepreneurs, has very pertinent experiences about how skip managers can make or break organizations. Hence, there is an urgent need to disseminate knowledge on this aspect so that FTMs in big corporates, start-ups or SMEs understand skip management the right way and become facilitators in building great companies. We also come across students specializing in Human Resources (HR), Organizational Behaviour (OB) and Learning and Development (L&D), who are generally clueless about skip situations and lack the ability to handle them. Hence, to make them mindful of the realities of skip management while still in classrooms, this book will serve as their own personal north star.

Picture this for a while: A person joins the team of a project manager in a progressive company. On the day of induction, the skip manager comes to the new joinee and in front of the whole department tells him: Hey Joe, for the next two months, you are my apprentice. Let me coach you on the best ways to deliver at a workplace. Joe looks at his immediate boss and then the skip manager and begins his first day at work confused about the authority on the floor. Good skip managers never assign tasks to employees two levels below them; but then, not all managers make good skip managers.

Life presented me with experiences both as reporting to a skip manager and being a skip manager myself, and I continue to have such experiences while coaching and mentoring first time managers. I left two jobs specifically because I did not like the manager I was reporting to and took up a new job due to the good credentials of the skip manager. I did not let my previous experiences of reporting to bad managers cloud my judgement while accepting the next assignment.

There are new-age organizations where an employee's ability to have a positive influence in an organization from any hierarchical standpoint is respected and hence remains relevant. During one of my management roles, the induction of a new managing director (MD) transformed an underperforming organization to an aspiring one and it remains so even today. At the CXO level, I also got an opportunity to execute a positive turn-around of departments and eventually had a positive influence on the organization as a whole.

While everyone prefers to read inspiring stories of leadership, there are organizations whose expiry date is set in stone due to the conflicting messages given to teams by their immediate managers and skip managers.

In my 20 years in the corporate world and six years of coaching and consulting engagements in OB, career transitions and effective managerial skills, I have witnessed that skip-level leaders can and do have an extremely negative impact on an organization; this is something that isn't always taken seriously by the organization leaders. I have come across senior leaders, whom one can mistake for being light-hearted and packing a punch during conversations, but who, during coffee table or general interaction with employees two levels below, deliver sarcastic one-liners, leaving the employees and their managers disheartened and defeated as opposed to inspired. Employees, who are the receiving end of such veiled rebukes, frequently leave their jobs, citing the behaviour of skip-level managers as a reason for leaving; however, the feedback is never really acted upon and generally treated as an exit interview formality by the companies.

In this book, you will read in detail about skip management, its highs and lows, positives and pitfalls, based on the experiences of Stanford LEAD and MIT alumni across the world and other global leaders.

UNCHARTED WATERS: MY MANAGERIAL EXPERIENCES JUMPING THE CROSS-INDUSTRY SHIP

Employees should be presented with the purpose and objective they wish to attain as a part of the organization, before one wants them to walk the path to fulfil their manager's objectives and expectations. A few years after having entered the work force, I braved the unruly waters and applied for a role in a company that had nothing to do with the work experience I already had; the company offered none of the products or services I had already worked with earlier. Initially, I felt like a fish out of water, but gradually I accepted my choice. My first week at the company, I had to deal with the phrase 'pin drop silence', first-hand. The existing team was not sure why they should talk to or take orders from someone hired from a background, completely unrelated to the work they were doing. My first few weeks in office completely lacked any kind of action and sitting in office, hour after hour, without any interaction became desultory. I continued to read about the new industry, hoping to learn enough to provide direction to my team. On the social aspect, I wished someone would invite me to join them for lunch. However, it seemed like I was a wallflower, completely unnoticed. I didn't lose hope and waited patiently for some movement from my team's end. The person who hired me was my immediate manager; he always motivated me and assured me of my ability to lead the team, but on the other hand he continued to lead my reportees and kept poking them to take instructions from him. I became aware of this within six months into the organization. One day, sometime during those six months, I received a mail in my inbox; it was a resignation email from one of the teammates. It is hard to imagine that I had not even gotten to know my team and the exits had already begun. I took a deep breath, thought for a while and replied to that mail, asking the person to come over for a discussion. He came in and casually told me that he had been aspiring for my position and since the company preferred to hire an outsider, he decided to put in his resignation papers. During the first 15 minutes of our conversation, I realized that this person had a plethora of knowledge of the industry and was only three years away from retirement. The more surprising element was that he had already discussed his resignation with my reporting manager, that is, his skip manager. I understood why he was not given my job but was stiff baffled about why my manager was still guiding a team that reported to me, albeit on paper for now. There were two challenges for me now; one was to retain this person and other was to give him a perception of authority, which ensured that the umbilical cord between the team and the skip manager was subtly severed. Trying to hook this person, I suggested to him that we co-create ideas for the team and make his last three years in the corporate world, the highest point of his life. I tried to seal the deal by pointing out the practical aspect of sticking to this company, that it will not be easy to get another job at his age, which was close to retirement. Further, I tried to make him see that he would rather have an enterprising three years ahead than waste these years looking for a different opportunity. This thought struck a chord with him and he mulled over his decision while I watched him intently. Eventually, after few more platitudes and a discussion about my plans for the team and his role in executing those plans, we shook hands and I agreed to delete his resignation email. He acted as the team anchor for three years and ensured that the team delivered and overachieved targets. During these years, my manager had tried to approach my team a few times to guide them, however, my reportees ensured that they stuck to our team plan and not get swayed by the one their skip manager was imposing on them. I left the company after three years of hard work, having built a strong B2B business model for the companies' products and services. Looking back, I feel I left the company unscathed from any professional damage, in fact, I got more proficient in handling skip management politics.

EXPERIENCES OF SAUL JAEGER AS A POLICE CAPTAIN AND A SKIP MANAGER

Saul is a Stanford LEAD alumnus and a police captain at the Mountain View Police Department, San Francisco Bay Area. Saul is a very impactful leader and helps in making the community safer. In his line of work, Saul deals with complex criminal investigations, traffic collision, crime scene reconstructions, crisis negotiations, etc. In order to maintain a good relationship with the community at large, Saul leverages his social media, public relations and counselling skills. He also remains at the top of technology advents like autonomous vehicles and unmanned aircraft systems. We discussed certain stress situations, pertaining to skip managers, that were related to me by a few FTMs. To my surprise, Saul said that such situations are prevalent in his job as well. My curiosity got the better of me and I probed him to tell me his experiences as well as experiences of other professionals in his field, with skip managers. Here is what Saul had to say.

Law enforcement utilizes a hierarchical, paramilitary and ranked based structure. This is based on the need for a clear command structure (chain of command) and decision-making, well-defined mission parameters and goals as well as specific and easy to understand functions during an emergency or a critical incident. However, there are times, during those critical incidents, where skip management is worthwhile and adds value and can sometimes, even be necessary. On the other hand, it can also backfire, slow things down and devalue autonomous thinking and overall morale.

As a manager, Saul struggled most when he believed he knew exactly what needs to get done and how it needs to get done. He recalled how he used to hear voices in his head telling him to 'just do it yourself' and 'you can do it faster and correctly'. Even so, he would fight the urge every single time and found, through many years of experience, that the outcome is much, much greater when he let others perform under his guidance. In his current role, Saul manages several other managers, who, in turn, oversee direct supervisors, who take charge of line level staff. The urge mentioned above, presents itself very often, especially when he interacts with employees who report to his subordinates, or his subordinates' subordinates. In his world, generally, there are two times when this happens; during an event, organically, or at a planned event. In the event of the latter, one is prepared and can plan and account for potential morale issues, ego problems, etc. The former is a bit more dangerous because of the potential for influencing decisions based on formal rank, challenging egos and creating a divisive and negative work environment.

What Saul found most effective in dealing with such situations was to be extremely aware of when an opportunity presents itself organically, that is, the most challenging of situations, then taking the time to weigh all, or as many, of the potential outcomes of interfering with the specific task at hand. If such an opportunity presents itself when dealing with a critical incident like leading a team of officers into an active school shooting incident, then yes, Saul chooses to direct and (skip) manage the team, regardless of organizational roles or where people fall in an organizational chart. They have a job to do and direct action is required. However, if the situation presents itself when Saul is acting as the overall incident commander, being fed information from a variety of sources and making decisions about the overall mission, relying on other managers to guide their teams based on Saul's direction, then Saul chooses to depend on his subordinates to manage their respective teams and utilizes his time to gather intelligence and make decisions based on additional expertise and experience.

In certain sectors where life can be at risk, like chemicals, oil and gas or law enforcement, skipping the chain of command is required at times. However, the stone one drops in the water may have a bigger ripple effect than anticipated in the immediate future and time to come.

There are occasions when first time supervisors and skips sit together with their subordinates in order to brainstorm: This usually happens when the issues at hand are complex and large scale. An example of such a situation is a team meeting scheduled to discuss how the police force could reduce the number of automobile burglaries occurring throughout the city. In this meeting, regardless of rank, the new supervisors and the experienced ones like Saul, should create a collaborative and essentially flat environment for everyone to feel comfortable sharing ideas and experiences with the goal of developing a holistic solution to the problem.

I was very intrigued to learn from Saul about his experiences with his skip manager, in order to advise the FTMs that I was coaching on the problem situations they were encountering in their position as FTMs. Saul provided me with very thought-provoking insights.

When skip management is done 'correctly', it can be very effective, but like most things, if not done well/correctly, it can cause more problems than solve. This is very true in the law enforcement world, a world in which the chain of command is paramount for survival and safety. Saul has experienced being skip-managed poorly. He has felt, first-hand, the various emotions caused by this experience which he later conveyed to me during our various conversations on this topic. First and foremost is a feeling of not being trusted or that his supervisor doesn't trust Saul's work. A very close second is a feeling of autonomy being pulled out from under Saul. Lastly, there is a feeling of frustration, sadness and lack of motivation.

Looking back, these feelings arose mostly during more critical incidents. Saul recalls, as a mid-level manager, having his boss directing his reportees. Although Saul believes that he knows now this was not done nefariously, in fact it was more about the demon he mentioned previously, sitting on their shoulder shouting, it still stung, and still stings today. This goes back to his point about the potential negative side of skip management; done poorly, the effects can last a long time.

Taking a cue from Saul's experiences, I can remember one of my own experiences with a skip manager. I was working with a third-level leader in a Fortune 500. This person had received many complaints over the years about his abusive, sarcastic and punitive leadership across levels. However, his manager did nothing about it, the subordinates were silent, and the HR was not concerned. He remained in that level of authority for almost six years and his reportees and skip juniors changed almost every year due to the high attrition rate from his team. From his skewed leadership, I understood that exceptional skip leaders are the ones who are balanced in their praises and rebukes, who hold people accountable and make all their subordinates, whether direct or indirect, feeling respected and relevant.

Here's the truth about skip leadership handling first time managers: As one grows in an organization, they can get complacent and start taking things for granted, however, to be an effective skip leader one must have the right balance of authority, influence and soft skills. If not done well, the FTMs suffer and even their teams have nowhere to go. Ultimately, situations concerning skip leadership can become a difficult terrain and a slippery one too, for which no one prepares and guides FTMs.

HOW TO MAKE THE TRANSITION SUCCESSFUL

Let's look at how the transition of professionals from ICs to FTMs can be made successful; this is a critical juncture in one's career. The managerial role offers a sense of pride to the candidate. Little does he or she know that the role may not be a good fit for them. Becoming a manager shouldn't be a sign of social relevancy. However, there are psychological pressures, like gaining acceptance and respect from peers and society or a need for money that make people accept managerial positions even though they might be better suited to individual contributor roles.

In order to have a successful transition, one must understand the leadership style they want to emulate. The catch here is that leadership styles need to adjust in accordance with the working style of one's team. Hence, an FTM needs to tweak his strategies with the changing team patterns in order to get the best out of everyone in his or her team.

To allow the readers to make use of the different personalities a leader may possess, the author has decoded the various leadership styles through this book. The different personas of a leader are the master, the prober, the skipper, the assembler, the boilerplate, the fort and the star gazer. Regardless of being an FTM or a skip manager, one can develop leadership agility to be better at their job and feel more confident.

The different leadership personalities have been briefly discussed below.

THE MASTER

The master leadership personality denotes professionals who are subject-matter experts, established as thought leaders and have lot of data and experience to back their decisions. This leadership style works with employees who have recently begun their professional careers. In this kind of a setup, the manager experiences a high school like environment. The manager may find the team feeling directionless as these co-workers are yet to understand how to navigate the corporate world. In this light, the role of the manager is truly like a master of the house. Such new-age workers in their early years of career are also digital addicts and have a need for fast paced action. It's their innate urge to keep checking their social media accounts even while attending important meetings. A successful master manager knows where to draw the line between mentorship and friendship in a professional setup; he knows when to let a 'toe out of line' slide and when to confront the rule-breaker.

THE PROBER

Probers rely on their ability to question the status quo and challenge their reportees to foster creativity and better-thinking. This managerial style works with a team that has smart and confident participants and can be guided to a higher level of greatness. The prober helps the team get access to resources to tackle their tasks and achieve substantial goals. The prober relies on this questioning to create a culture of inspiration and fun; probers prefer to take on single-priority objectives rather than tackling a multitude of priorities at the same time, which may leave even a smart team, confused.

THE SKIPPER

The skipper, as the name suggests, works like a team captain. The skipper ensures that during day-to-day working also every team member is seen, engaged and heard. They build great relationships with every member of the group and understand that everyone is not an all-rounder. If the team has mixed talent and competence, a skipper is all they need to bring out the best in them. So, what does it take to be a skipper? It's happens quite often in a team that certain employees don't realize that their contribution matters and impacts the organization. In such a case, a skipper has to ensure that everyone in the team has a sense of purpose and believes that their efforts matter. The skipper assigns daily tasks to everyone in the team and makes sure that each employee knows how the task aids the company in reaching its goals. It makes work more meaningful and engaging.

THE BOILERPLATE

A manager displaying boilerplate leadership is sometimes referred to as the impossible boss. He is defined by quality work, discipline, accountability and setting hard-to-achieve goals. This type of leadership works well with a team that believes that the manager wants them to excel by going the extra mile and that the incentives for stretching themselves hard are huge. The boilerplate manager empowers the team to manage their energy and adrenaline more than managing their time. These managers make the team perform work that requires analytical and hard thinking when they are at their most alert and hence aligns the tasks to be performed to the productivity clocks of the team. In light of the inflexibility of time and non-negotiable deadlines, they try to achieve incredible results with a resilient team by motivating them to do more in the least amount of time.

THE ASSEMBLER

An assembler personality in a professional setup retains the characteristics of the assembler from whom this personality derives its name, that is, an assembler who works in factory shop floor. An assembler recognizes the tasks at hand and works with multiple belts and plates from various domains, moving at the same time, to make the final product. An assembler personality thrives best in a cross functional team and vice versa. The assembler mentors individual employees, increasing the quality and quantity of work they perform as a team from various divisions and geographies. This type of leadership works well with a team that's malleable and willing to accept an advisory approach.

THE STARGAZER

'Autonomy to be awesome' has been practised by corporates for some time now. However, if skilled professionals are bored of routine work, then more than autonomy, they need a vision—a vision of the next Mount Everest to climb. Here is what a stargazer does to materialize this vision. He develops a 'dare to dream' approach to help and align the team to long-term goals, has an experimental mindset and does not let ideas get snubbed. If voices in a team fall silent, then there is definitely something wrong. This managerial style works well with a few skilled idealists in the team struggling to improve and grow from where they currently are. Such a team is always on the lookout for their next brainchild; they thrive in the environment of constant anxiety as felt by new mothers. The stargazer ensures that the team is motivated by an urge for novelty and that all ideas originate from the team so that the sense of achievement lasts longer.

THE FORT

Consider an organization, which by nature of work and culture, is quite hierarchical—there can be potential outliers who are bogged down by routines and processes. To form a dependable team, in such a setup, needs structure, process frameworks and clarity to perform, which only a manager like a fort can provide—a protector, patient, solid, has the patience to wait for more information and understand the team's perspective before taking a decision and who likes to practice management routines along with keeping pace with new-age interventions. This type of leadership focusses on clarity over control and ensures respect at every hierarchical level and delegates to even the lowest level of the team to empower them in order to bring a positive change in ways of working.

In light of the above discussion, it is evident that all managers have to pivot between different managerial styles because their team members have multiple working styles. Effective management requires a quick flit-in and flit-out of the various personalities to correspond to the personality of the members of the team.

REVIEWER AND REVIEWEE

As an individual contributor, one has to only communicate horizontally with peers and vertically with superiors. However, the graduation from IC to FTM adds another axis of communication, which is downwards. The interplay between communicating in all three directions isn't as easy as it seems because the ones reporting to a manager are also judging him.

Many managers are not able to correct their working style because they don't get frequent feedback. In the absence of feedback and lack of course correction, the other employees keep negatively assessing the managerial abilities of the person and form an opinion based on such assessment without the manager getting a chance to improve. In case of managers being in other countries and separated from their reportees by time zones, it may take a bit longer, but eventually the reportees are able to judge the effectiveness of the manager in leading the team. As managers believe that it is their job to evaluate and assess the people reporting to them, they don't realize that the team is also evaluating their value to the team.

It is quite important as an FTM that when a negative feedback is received, it is not dismissed unceremoniously; it is vital that a serious assessment is carried out if a particular negative feedback is being received daily. The same feedback received again and again from different sources is not usually fabricated, in fact, it is probably true. When ICs become FTMs, they become defensive very early in the managerial life cycle. It's the dilemma of owning someone else's performance, good and bad, versus their own contribution to the organization. Getting defensive and deflective doesn't change how the team members view a manager's capabilities. An FTM has to create a realistic sense of trust and safety, especially when the FTM is managing the same team he or she was a part of before being promoted.

Some managers choose to pass the blame and wash their hands off the responsibility of a bad decision taken by one of his team members; however, the relief is short lived. Managers who often pass the blame of bad decisions stagnate the system. The overall actions of the managers define whether the team and organization at large will be engaging and efficient or not—a manager's actions define the organization's engagement and productivity.

Let us now look at the learning elements one must pay heed to when transitioning from and IC to an FTM in order to excel in the new role.

A FORMAL STRUCTURE

Uncertainty and a lack of structure is the most common mistake an individual contributor makes on being promoted to a managerial position. It's an oversight that should be avoided from day one. In the early days of elevation, a new manager oversees very few reportees; in such a case it might feel odd to put a structure of engagement in place. However, it's a habit to be inculcated early in one's managerial practices. Even if there are one or two reportees, it is relevant to ensure that there is a formal structure involving internal meetings and how they are conducted, for instance, maintaining a designated calendar for such meetings. It might be awkward at first, since the new reportees might be peers, however, clarity of thought and actions is important for the long haul.

An FTM should start with a meeting that sets the tone for the time to come; convey his or her vision to the team and also make known the fact that he or she would be in-charge of setting priorities for the team.

An FTM should also conduct one-on-one meetings at least once a week, but he or she should be sure not to spend majority of the team's time in conference rooms. It is enough to sit and talk in an informal environment on a daily basis, however, one formal weekly engagement is necessary to keep people on their toes. Further, it is considered a good practice to conduct one team meeting in a week if the new manager has more than one direct reportees.

CULTURE AND CONTEXT

Creating the right work culture in your micro-setup is the most important aspect of team performance and productivity. The morale of your team will depend a lot on the attitude and the tone you exhibit while interacting with them. The new manager can begin with letting the reportees know what he or she would want the team to be known for—what will be the pride of their division or team. Another good start would be to make each team member believe that they are the best persons for the goals the team has to accomplish, and any work done by them will be done to achievable perfection. Such positive messages will not only allow the manager to fit into the new role, but also motivate the team members as well as other employees to aspire to become contributing members of this 'dream team'. The new manager must ensure that the context is set such that the team knows they are a part of something bigger—the manager may begin with a clear articulation of the short-term and long-term goals. This would lead the team to be much more productive and effective.

SELF-ACCOUNTABILITY

The new manager has an uphill task making the reportees believe that they are in capable and responsible hands. As the manager's career has taken the next step in the corporate ladder, everyone in the team also expects to grow over a period of time. This means that the manager has to own poor team performance, have tough discussions during appraisals and adequately reward high performers. The team must believe that the new manager is slowly but steadily gaining control over responsibilities and is taking ownership of the tasks performed, good or bad. Being accountable as a new manager means to be an advocate for the team as well as represent the team in the parts and plays of the organization that are out of reach of the individual contributors.

PERFORMANCE MANAGEMENT

Every FTM knows they need to evaluate performance of their teams and it's an important aspect. The manager must know that fair treatment is not the same as equality: The rewards don't have to be split equally in a team, and neither are reprimands. An FTM should take time to understand what motivates individual team members and personalize the stimulus to get higher order performances. As a new manager, a professional should make a list of tasks and team members and assign multi-person projects and one-person projects basis the result to be achieved by the collective effort of the project team and the individual, respectively—Effort should be made to assign tasks that are complimentary to a person's unique strengths. If one has to make the team strive for improvement, it's important to give visibility and positive accolades to high achievers in front of the other divisions and skip-level managers. Many FTMs get entangled in their own dilemmas so much so that they forget to make two-way feedback a regular process. Ensure that your team knows, preferably in real time, about how you perceive their progress and correct the course in time, if needed.

Other common aspects to be dealt with as FTMs, are controlled nerves, not reacting to your own dilemmas in front of the team and taking ownership over the team completely.

LEARNING FROM THE INDUSTRY LEADERS

In the interview below, Mr Anil Nair, managing director of CISCO (Asia Pacific & Japan), discusses some of the issues faced by individual contributors and FTMs and skip-level managers.

Question 1: What are the challenges faced by individual contributors transitioning into FTMs and skip managers?

Soldiers becoming leaders. When you are in a front-line role, you are used to upward communication and reporting to the management. Suddenly, in a managerial role, you have both upward and downward management; handling both at the same time is a very sensitive task and needs finesse. Usually a good individual performer promoted ahead of the curve becomes a manager, and he deals with the sudden exposure to the corporate part of the organization per se. A manager might be asked to handle an entirely new business unit of which he/she may not have prior experience.

While working with Bradma India Ltd., Anil got promoted within two years of joining and was asked to lead the services unit. The people Anil was asked to lead were either peers or persons senior to him.

Establishing credibility and value in such situations becomes critical, especially when there isn't enough time. A popular belief is that a junior with lesser experience, cannot lead effectively—credibility is established by one's skill level and the management's trust on the person's ability to execute. Developing interpersonal skills for survival is what the IC does, however, in an FTM position, these skills are needed for getting the team efficiency. Self-introspection, control points, what to delegate and what not to delegate become very critical. New skills need to be developed and augmented, which starts with understanding people as much as understanding yourself. Along with self-evaluation, the sense to evaluate others has to be developed quickly. So, for an FTM, the journey is not in isolation; the FTM grows with the team and frequently requires help from the higher levels. Being disciplined and honest is important. If the team feels you are bluffing, it leads to an immediate loss of credibility. As an FTM, the team keeps looking up to you for leading by example so that the expectations of performance are set. If the FTM slacks by even 5 per cent, the team slacks five times that, therefore, it is very important to set a brisk pace for yourself and the team.

Question 2: How can skip managers make or break the organization culture?

When a person gets promoted, many organizations don't explain the new expectations. In such circumstances, the skip manager is not able to relinquish the team's control to the new manager and continues to manage. The newly promoted manager ends up being quite confused about his role. In such cases, the skip ends up leading the team just as he was doing earlier, and the middle manager is confused about his role. If the new manager is prepared well to take charge of the new assignment and gets enough time to communicate with the team, the skip level can then remain at a strategic level and may not need to get involved in tactical decision-making and day-to-day operations of the team. The new manager, if he/she gets time to settle down, can channelize the right communication as needed by the skip level and not practice tactical operational reporting. The earlier manager, who now moves to the skip level, might be measuring team performance by the time they spend at their desks; however, the new manager might be evaluating the team based on performance over time at work. So, breaking the skip-level set routines itself is a change of authority and the worst situation is such where the skip knows that he will always be able to take credit of the work done by the middle manager and gain laurels from the management. Skip managers can add value by being strategic advisors and break the organizations by being too interfering at lower levels and taking credit of their work for their own gains.

Question 3: What are the dos and don'ts when thinking about jumping over the boss's head?

In the Indian context, having a moral compass is subjective. Shortcuts are never the way to succeed. If one jumps over the boss's head and make the boss defensive, it's possible the boss may shoot in any direction to get the person down on his/her knees. Along the way, people manipulate the management to make use of the company resources for personal gains. People upend their professional priorities by working to keep friends happy, the team happy and the company happy, in that order. The person going over the boss's head must keep the boss informed, even if after the fact. If you are right in your assessment, you should never be apprehensive about calling out the boss to the top management. When you jump levels, the middle managers generally become insecure, some not for any particular reason; mostly insecurity arises when managers take credit for other's work and the bluff is called out when the skip talks to the managers' reportees. Effective communication and using reasonable and impartial language when jumping levels, is very critical. Further, the reception may also depend on the whether the higher management is aligned among themselves such that the person who goes over his/her boss's head is not caught in a crossfire. There is no surety that the person being reached out to will act in line or just ignore the complaint.

Question 4: What are the issues that arise when multi-locational/multicultural teams are to be handled? How to minimize miscommunication and mitigate the challenges?

Working with team members separated by geography, needs a time-sensitive approach, else a manager will be left taking midnight calls and decisions. Saying 'Please do it', might be considered appropriate in a certain culture, while in another culture, it may be viewed as rudely assertive. Professionals in some countries have an inherent feeling of superiority over professionals of other countries, in terms of work and lineage. This complex starts to reflect in a person's tone and language and dealing with this becomes important. Any leeway in this can affect the manager's credibility. In some cultures, if you are five minutes late, your credibility may get hurt and your juniors may dismiss you as manager. You can't also be seen to be friendlier with employees from your own clan/community/country. Another shortcoming of distance-working is when some professionals imitate the each other's cultures, for instance, a European professional may greet his manager saying *namaste*: The problem arises where the manager doesn't know whether the greeting is cordial or sarcastic. Irrespective of the culture and geographical location of an employee, it is essential to be straightforward with colleagues and focused on the task at hand. Filter through what needs to be done and what can be let off. One must focus on resolving conflicts that might be surfacing rather than creating more conflicts. Sometimes accents and repetitive requests to clarify can become offensive: You may not want a Japanese to lead a Korean market.

Question 5: What are the challenges faced by managers when the team grows in number?

The moment you assume a new position that makes you responsible for a large team, it is crucial to know exactly where the team is placed at that moment and what needs to be done to bring the team where you want it to be. As such, keeping informed and taking necessary action are both important when managing large teams. A standard way to begin your managerial career is to establish a transparent system of communication, which can be achieved through team meetings or conference calls. As a manager the amount of preparation that is needed to take decisions is very high. The manager can utilize the team meetings and calls to steer focus in the direction he has envisaged for the team; the manager can also keep the reportees on their toes by inquiring about productivity and progress, one person at a time.

The manager may have to tackle language and accent barriers if the teams are operating from different geographies. This issue may be effectively tackled by communicating over emails more than discussing over calls. If a meeting is unavoidable, the tone and speed of words can be modulated to communicate effectively. Sometimes, the calls may last for 6–8 hour. With minor tweaks, such long calls can be faster and more effective. When this suggestion was placed on the table, the management was quite worried about bringing about such changes. However, with a common format and clear objective, the rambling was reduced, and the calls were finally managed in 2 hours flat: no scope for people to waylay the calls since everything on the template is factual. There is a learning curve when it comes to managing large teams. Sometimes, everything is not relevant for everyone.

Maintaining regular communication and contact is very important once the team starts growing in number. As teams grow, the manager also needs to cut the flab and avoid duplication of work and responsibilities. Clarity of roles is also very important in such situations. It's not limited to just setting out an agenda and speaking about it. More importantly there is the need for follow-up on actions agreed to during review meetings and strategy discussions. Growing large teams is not like a classroom for attendance taking, it's about asking the right question and ensuring that the teammate has an answer next time. That qualifies for action more than follow-ups. If teams grow and manager spend time only in follow-ups, then the next level inflection in performance is difficult to achieve.

Question 6: How strong are executive isolation dynamics in organizations and why? Why do managers try to keep their bosses isolated from the teams?

In a progressive organization, everyone should be able to talk to everyone. Executive isolation is a sign of an insecure manager. Managers must facilitate skip-level discussions rather than employ executive isolation practices. The number of people approaching the managers for operational assistance and tactical work must be moderated. That way the team becomes more independent and the manager gets time to work on strategy and resources.

Question 7: What is the impact of managers getting friendly with reportees and then not being able to detach themselves from the reportees after becoming skip managers? How can confusion caused by parallel authorities be avoided?

Skip level is not always connected to the ground and the middle manager must not be a showstopper. As a unit head one should not have restrictions on talking to different members of his or her team, whichever level they are at. However, good managerial practices obligate the skip to always keep the middle manager in the loop, both during formal and informal meetings and chats with a junior, who directly reports to the middle manager. Then again, subordinate managers must recognize the inevitability of skips and his reportees talking once in a while without his knowledge. As such, the manager must contend with any insecurity he may have, prioritizing the good of the company, the team and himself/herself, in that order. The manager should ensure that the team is more aligned with him rather than the skip managers. The manager's ability to shape a team outdoes a skip's, even though the skip has more authority. A team chooses who to listen to depending on who is making more sense. Ultimately, credibility always wins. Since, age is not a factor anymore to decide who becomes a manager, it is experience, professional relevance and the ability to take positive action, which is important to maintain credibility.

Question 8: How do leadership teams create better managers? Whether leaders should always take charge of business strategies and/or solutions or display the ability to question, listen and learn from their teams?

Leaders should see, seek and harvest. They should put all their experience on the table and then inculcate progressive thinking. An effective leader should have a developed antenna to identify the professionals who are young in years but old of wisdom, so that professionals who are better at their job get their due. A role complementing the personalities of the team members will help get the work done faster and better. The leaders, while they must be very good listeners, should also be able to seed the right thoughts and actions in the team such that the expected results can be harvested in time. Leaders need to earn the respect due to them and leaders should let the teams have a share in the achievements of the organizations. One can't lead if others don't follow. It is important to effectively use the available information; merely possessing the information doesn't help.

FURTHER READINGS

'7 Leadership Styles the Best Bosses Use (Just Not All at Once).' https://www.forbes.com/sites/dailymuse/2016/04/21/7-leadership-styles-the-best-bosses-use-just-not-all-at-once/#2d2d84922cae

DECODING EFFECTIVE BUSINESS STRUCTURES AND HIERARCHIES

THE HIERARCHICAL CONUNDRUM

MULTICULTURAL, MULTI-LOCATIONAL WORKPLACE PERSPECTIVE

Almost all organizations have a set hierarchical structure for running different processes like planning, staffing, budgeting and evaluating outcomes, well. However, it is important that such structures are flexible enough to transform as per the needs of external and internal stakeholders, rather than expecting the stakeholders to change in line with the organization structures. The future workplace doesn't have boundaries, only the right integration elements to be able to manage teams that are multi locational and multicultural. Due to self-imposed structures, frameworks and boundaries, many organizations are not able to fully exploit the potential of the staff across locations. The essence of successful operation of the company across different cultures and locations is ensuring that hierarchical structures and work habits prevalent in one culture or country are not blindly replicated in other cultures and countries without accounting for cultural adjustments. Appropriate organization structure can help managers in assessing and managing the performance of the teams better, especially if they are spread across cultures and geographies. Understanding the company structure can ensure setting up of proper authority guidelines for linking organizational goals to operational goals to be achieved by individuals team members.

Organizations, by and large, function on one of the two types of structures: military and sports. What's common to both these types of structures is discipline, commitment and performance. Depending on the age of the company and the expected team size, the management can decide which structure to adapt and when.

Military Structure

Military structure is a traditional structure on which companies continue to function; it places the decision-makers (critical and analytical thinkers) at top of the pyramid and battle troops or the doers, comprising of entry level and mid-level employees, at the bottom. The structure works when the employees at the front line obey the decision-makers at the top. They have the autonomy to set their day-to-day agenda, however, they lack any power to take tactical decisions affecting the company. The structure works on directives and authority where superiors must have tactical information about what is happening on a day-to-day basis in the company in order to make decisions and inform the teams below on how to execute. There is a distinct line between the various levels in the company as well as a conventional way in which employees and the top management interact with one other. Such structures supersede seniority over purpose. Sometimes such structures inhibit a quick response to competitive moves. Being a lateral structure, everyone will need to be informed about the requirement to counter competition. Once the information is made available to relevant levels, then their speed of response becomes critical to the actions. Due to multi-level information sharing protocols and possible delays in the process of decision-making, the question on agility of this structure surfaces quite often.

In the early 1990s, IBM was a highly profitable organization. However, by 1993, the consumer needs and behaviours had changed so much that IBM was on its way to incur USD 16 billion in losses. IBM went on to be on a watch list for extinction and was desperate to have a leader that could orchestrate a turnaround. It was amidst this structural and business crisis that Louise Gerstner Jr was brought in to run IBM. IBM had been becoming victim of its lumbering size and insular corporate culture when Louis V. Gerstner Jr took charge of the company and turned it around. The challenges and how IBM overcame them are very well-articulated in the book *Who Says Elephants Cannot Dance* written by Louise V. Gerstner Junior, who served as chairman and chief executive officer of IBM from April 1993 till he retired in March 2002. The author claims that the company was victimized by its own size, its slow pace of decision-making, a complacent corporate culture and the advent of personal computers and laptops era. He also talks about how the elephant finally let go of the inertia of processes and developed a collaborative working culture to take on the new world order.

The industry thought Lou Gerstner was coming in to dissolve the big giant into smaller units since IBM could not adequately react to the challenges from competitors in the marketplace. But Lou didn't want to make an organization that was credited with many important technological inventions and patents, face extinction.

Detailed in the book is a real-life account of what changed the fortunes for IBM: Gerstner began with creating a balance between the traditional military structure and the collaborative sports structure. He made sure that the company strategy was developed and implemented at a level playing field, where everyone could see where the ball was. He ensured that the managers worked together to solidify the company's mission as a customer focused 'service provider', which heralded their exit from the hardware product business. Gerstner secured the company's existence by making certain that the management took quick pricing and market positioning decisions, keeping the competition at bay. Under a different management, this change might have taken to happen at IBM.

Who Says Elephants Can't Dance talks about how the right interventions at the right time in hierarchical structures of companies leads to a competitive and cultural transformation? It starts with rebuilding trust in the leadership by ensuring that everyone in the organization, from the CEO to the janitor, has a common and renewed sense of purpose. The book is an extraordinary story about how structures and hierarchies can be altered for the benefit of an organization, while reflecting on where the industry is headed, in order to better align the principals of leadership. Such decisions involve high stakes. Most times, if a company waits too long to make a decision, or avoids a certain course for a long time, they end up with no recourse at all and have to face the consequences of the inaction. There are many companies that shut down because they didn't use hierarchies to their advantage in a multi-locational and multicultural setup: IBM was not one of them. They came out from the dark rather than becoming a shadow of their extant status.

Sports-like Structures

While military structures are vertical, the new-age structures do not have well-defined hierarchies, instead they work how sports are played. Imagine a football field or a cricket ground: Everyone is on a level playing arena with their eye on the prize, which signifies common objectives, clearly defined roles, timely back-up, with the employees working like a well-oiled machine. The environment may be informal and sometimes involves crude language; however, it is meant to be all in good faith. In this structure, competence precedes authority and that's what makes the organization more agile, though processes may get compromised once in a while.

Sports structures are followed by organizations that are more purpose driven than hierarchy sensitive. The hierarchy is only kept enough in order to maintain discipline.

Hierarchy in this organizational structure is the new management cannon that recognizes the paradigm of new-age leadership and management in what is referred to as the Creative Economy.

The structure allows for an uninterrupted flow of information and communication of responsibilities, not dependent on levels of authorities. Consider what happens when someone calls the Amazon customer care service and registers a complaint: The executive, at his level, has the authority to offer you a refund even though you may be expecting a long-drawn battle to convince the company to give your money back. In doing so, the executive saves the company's time and effort that is needed to make customers more loyal.

The sports structure leads to corner offices and business battle fields to be better connected in terms of engagement and collaboration. The structure is defined by inclusion and participation more than hoarding and authority.

A few years ago, I was reading Jack Welch's *Straight from the Gut* for the second time and I realized how it was so ahead of its time. Jack started with General Electric (GE) straight out of college and went onto retire as Chairman, not to mention how he changed the face of management practices and studies for the greater good.

His narrative elaborates about the management style adopted at GE in order to reduce work duplication and bureaucracy.

This also included the process that was followed to identify Jack's successor. He learnt there are no shortcuts and facts must be faced just like in a game of soccer, when a ball is hit by a goalkeeper, every player on the field knows the status and position of the ball. That is similar to organization structures where most things are transparent to teams and not on 'need to know basis'. Jack demonstrated the skill in risk-taking. He understood that losing a game is not the same as losing value for good. As a team on the sports field, Jack ensured that the organization lived in the present and was motivated by impeccable work ethics without any shortcuts. Jack held the elements of work ethics, motivation, tab on current events to be foremost. Jack also demonstrated the need for a proper coach to lead a team to victory. His efforts to put human development first, talks a lot about the person Jack was. In a sport, sometimes the most unexpected player performs well; the same can happen in an entrepreneurial set up: Jack was that person for creative problem-solving and on the spot improvisations.

In every new game, the initial moments are uncertain and watchful. This is exactly what Jack did and watched who in the organization had the mental acumen to brace the changes and induced turmoil. He developed what is known as the concept of 'soft values of excellence' that made people become more valuable assets. During the 1990s, when the world was going through a binary revolution, GE didn't take part in developing itself as a digital organization: They kept their eyes on the traditional game plan while the world was changing formats and rules of engagement to embrace digital transformations, new dimensions of technology and business models and fast paced decision-making.

Jack looked at four major foundations of business to make GE a new-age organization: global business access, right mix of products and services, quality par excellence and e-business. This is like a sports field where high-performing opponents are shadowed by other team members in order to try and hold them back from hitting home ground. Jack's plan included effective people management for managing costs, increasing revenues, expanding and diversifying the business to enhance efficiency and quality of outcomes.

Jack finally decided to be a coach rather than the team captain but had to find a successor to lead the team into the field. Jack believed that finding a worthy successor was one of the most difficult tasks of his career. He eventually found the man who maintained GE's winning streak and took them to new victories. It was a true integration between teams working from multiple locations across cultures and diversity.

KINDS OF BOTTLENECKS

Organizations are obsessed with creating a multicultural and multi-locational workforce; organizations want a global presence in the form of diverse managers and employees and manager. Despite the obsession, organizations recognize that it is difficult and painstaking to manage multicultural and multi-locational teams from a cohesive workplace perspective. Most managers fall short of the mark and skips are no exception. The urge to create a diverse team is very nice on paper, however, getting people from all walks of life, cultures and beliefs, and making them come together to share, create and implement new ideas is easier said than done. If not managed well, it can lead to a productivity disaster and impact business continuity. Managers often hear about the benefits of developing virtual and global organizations. Such elements, whilst they help paint an optimistic picture of diversity and globalization in the workplace, sometimes actually offer minor benefits as compared to the serious threat they can pose to organizations if mismanaged.

Many a times, global organizations are created for cost considerations, reducing time to market a new product or service or in other instances for reputation management, to position a company that can serve global clients. There is a striking difference between developing virtual global teams for the sake of equality in opportunity and doing it for the sake of effective performance.

Multi-locational teams, connected virtually, allow professionals to from a wide variety of backgrounds to become a part of teams and organizations, which theoretically sounds wonderful. How to manage this confluence successfully requires a whole new set of processes and actions from managers and skips. Some of the problems are discussed here.

1. The first problem faced by supervisors is that they are unable to satisfactorily explain the job requirements to people in a way they would understand best. People who are based out of different work zones perceive, experience and understand their profiles very differently. This makes it harder for managers to make staff work together effectively. Members of geographically and culturally diverse teams may have trouble agreeing on even simple tasks like interpreting and analysing data, in addition to the problems that arise due to time zone mix-ups and calendar mismatches.

2. The second problem has to do with the sense of solidarity and togetherness in the team. One gets a sense of team cohesion if they demonstrate a united front to achieve a common goal. Being a truly global team implies that not only group goals are met but team members in various geographies get

a sense of belonging and that their contribution is important for the overall objective of the project assigned to the team. As managers, it becomes mentally tiring to supervise teams in multiple geographies: Imagine waking up at 5 am (IST), ready to talk to the Singapore team shortly and then sleeping very late at night after briefing the teams in Sweden and UK. Even if the manager would like to give his best, the fatigue due to difference in time zones tires the manager's efforts and his or her team starts to fragment over a period of time. Moreover, if the team is highly diverse, the cohesive elements tend to be even lower. In such situations there are more conflicts which prove to be quite disastrous for productivity.

3. The third problem that arises is the problematic consequence of managers wanting to manage more. When managers forget to first manage the team issues at hand and focus more on increasing their sphere of influence by increasing the number of employees in their team, it leads to reluctance in team members to collaborate and share ideas due to the increase in competition. While managers believe that larger teams will have a great range of views, experiences and opinions, it may backfire since the teams stop sharing knowledge and information due to excessive competition.

So, what can managers and supervisors do to solve issues relating to managing large teams?

IDENTIFYING WITH EACH TEAM MEMBER

Firstly, the organizations must ensure that the managers know how to identify the right team members from multi-locational and multicultural aspects, who are likely to take pride in being a part of the team in the making. These team members should also be able to relate to the kind of tasks they are expected to perform. Dispelling the antagonistic feelings between team members, the manager needs to craft their thoughts to a collective future, goal and vision.

> The higher the geo and gender diversity of the team, the more crucial it becomes for the members to identify with the project in unison.

This is a very difficult task especially for FTMs who are either promoted within the organization or hired laterally.

The managers have to make sure that each member adds a specific and distinctive value to the team such that the skills don't overlap with one another. Like discussed above, accommodating team members from various geographies and cultures can become difficult for managers. The intent needs to be able to provide equal representation to the people in the team and respect them as individual contributors as much as a part of the team. Some team members will be better at cost management and others may be better at customer handling. Overall, the team will appear balanced, but each individual member must know that their contributions are important and respected.

Managers should inspire the teams to work together and not encourage negative competition withing the team. They should develop the spirit of 'healthy competition' amongst the team members and nurture them to be fiercely objective oriented. Managers mentioning that they are looking for the most creative way of problem-solving, leads to every person in the team aspiring to bring out their best. The manager must ensure that the team has the willingness to push boundaries to solve problems. Being adaptive and creative with no measurable outcome can drain the team and the manager, getting nothing out of them.

Being objective is the way to ensure there is healthy competition and no one goes behind anyone's back. For a fact, no one wants a job where they have to keep competing rather than collaborating. Hence, it's important to ensure that a competitive spirit isn't so overpowering that is brings down the morale of the team or leads to a stressful environment.

EMBRACING TEAM MEMBERS' WORK PRACTICES

The Remote Working Dilemma

Typically, most corporates in India practise flexi-hours but don't prefer the staff to be working from home (WFH). However, in Nordic countries WFH appears to be the most common work practice. If a manager is hardwired to a way of working, then embracing other colleagues' work practices can become difficult over time. If a manager based in India starts objecting to the option of work from home for the team operating from one of the Nordics, it will lead to a conflict.

According to a survey conducted by the *Society for Human Resource Management* in *2017* on Employee Benefits, 'more than 60 per cent of companies offer telecommuting benefits in USA and encourage work from home'. This can be attributed to organizations focusing on the results of the operation more than the location of operations. The traffic conditions in the world are worsening; it proves a deterrent to travel to office every day. With laptops and mobiles being very affordable, accessibility is not an issue, and neither is working anytime, anywhere during office hours. Further, many employees don't prefer to go into offices to get the job done. The reasons may be that they find home to be a safer place or they want to avoid distractions at the workplace. Many a times the meeting they need to attend with clients are closer to home than office hence commute to work makes no sense.

A manager with no experience to work from home may not be able to handle a team working from home. Similarly, there can be team members who have never worked from home and the manager may want them to. The effective handling of both situations will require due care by the manager.

Stanford professor, Nicholas Bloom, states that employees working from home are 13 per cent more productive. They also find it easier to concentrate because the employees can choose their work environment. For instance, I really enjoy working with loud music and would love to work in a place where music can be turned on; however, others may prefer a quieter work environment. Similarly, an extrovert member of the team may feel lonely and isolated working from home due to their lively and social nature while an introvert may thrive in such an environment.

As part of the aforementioned study, it was observed that employees who are allowed to work remotely are less likely to take sick days or rejuvenation breaks. Managers who encourage telecommuting know how it impacts project costs and timely delivery in a positive way.

OTHER GOOD MANAGERIAL PRACTICES

1. Understanding the behaviour and personalities of their team members.
2. In case of a replacement in the managerial position, the old manager should share his understanding of the team members personalities with the new manager.
3. As a skip manager, let the new manager mingle with the team without unnecessary interference, so that

> the team can independently align themselves with the personal disposition and vision of the new manager.
>
> 4. As a new manager, the first step should be to bond with your team members, to let them understand and get used to your managerial style.
>
> 5. In order to strike a balance between employees who prefer telecommuting and the ones that prefer working in office, managers can implement a 'team work day'. Team work days would involve everyone working from office, one or two days a week, so that the team gets to physically work together and bond.

Let us discuss the experiences of a versatile Ivy League college pass-out, with two decades of experience in the corporate field, who goes by the initials JD.

A few years ago, JD was leading a multi-locational team, which had an engineering and an operations arm. Each team was managed by their own managers. JD was a business unit leader responsible for business sustenance and enhancement, managing the P&L account, improving customer relationship as well as ensuring an increase in the life time value (LTV) of clients for the company. During his initial days on the program, his team was ridden with challenges every step of the way to success; he resolved these challenges using skip-level meetings. Below is a quick snapshot of how JD handled multicultural and multi-locational teams.

JD identified the issue as being that one team didn't appreciate the work done by the other teams. In effect, the enhancements made by development team were not accepted by the operations team and vice versa. The managers working under him started playing the blame game, leading to cultural enmity within the teams and JD, of course, bore the brunt of it from the end of the company as well as the customers. His 50-member team had different hierarchies, different skill levels and different cultural and geographical backgrounds. Even more serious than these problems were the 'information asymmetry and lack of individual identification to the overarching objectives' of the team and the company. Within a month from the day of joining the company, he was being threatened by the customer to terminate the contract. JD had never reached out to skip levels himself nor had he implemented such a process yet where his team needed to approach skip levels. Here is how he approached both the teams to manage the issues being faced by them.

- **Operations Team:** The operations team worked diligently 24x7 but focused only on their objectives as a team within a team without trying to understand the overall product or the intent behind it. One of the services the team was building was to provide One Time Password (OTP) service, which banks, e-commerce, insurance and telecom companies send to our phones. To enable the team members to overcome the problem of not receiving the OTP on time, JD tried to simplify the problem. To put things in perspective, he asked them to imagine a scenario where one billion people don't get an OTP. He implored to their sense of responsibility towards their work and told them that *the application they are supporting does the job of sending OTPs. When they do their job right, millions of people get OTPs on time.* Given their skill level, it was essential to be as succinct as possible and give a real-life view of the situation. JD understood that in order to motivate them to feel responsible for their work, it was essential to make them understand the value of their work; and that is what he did.

- **Development Team:** The developers focused on enhancements and building new features for the product. This team had an entirely different composition with folks bent on solving problems, thinking laterally, with an innovative and futuristic mindset. This team was under the impression that the product they developed would never have bugs and would work seamlessly without issues. This idea was promoted by their manager and they were also shielded from any pushback by their manager. However, the truth was that they needed to understand the operations team's perspective who were responsible for handling the issues arising in the real-time implementation of the product built by the development team. At a skip-level discussion with the whiz kids in the production team, JD tried to show them the working of the product holistically, which required them supporting the operations team.

The reaction to skip meetings across both teams was very encouraging. The results took a while to emerge but were quite unprecedented. People who had given up on the program, including JD's management, were pleasantly surprised. It ended well when clients renewed the contract as they were much satisfied with the company's performance.

On his part, JD got insight on his team members and how they spent eight hours of work effectively; he learned what motivates them to come to work each day, what they love and what they hate about the job. JD realized that teams might be able to overcome their bad experiences like long working hours and not being appreciated for their contributions if managers show empathy. JD's empathy for them led to them being empathetic toward their customers and eventually the consumers.

Managing a team working remotely is one of the unique challenges faced by managers but may prove an unavoidable way of conducting business. It's quite a logistical nightmare to put together a remotely working and multi-locational high-performing team. However, the right strategies can make it simple and effective. A team leader could be in San Francisco Bay Area managing teams in countries as disparate as Italy, Japan and Australia; that's three different continents, three different time zones, and myriad cultural differences that one cannot learn in the short term.

Taking a cue from JD's experience, here is what a manager should do if he wants to make progress in a remotely connected global team ecosystem.

Empathize

Stay connected, officially and informally, to get the work done. However, a line needs to exist between showing empathy to employees' problems and over-connecting with them.

New managers, who were more recently part of the team that they are to lead, often connect more with their teams even as managers considering there already exists some level of comfort and rapport between them. A manager must make the effort and express an interest in getting to know each team member and understand what is going on at their end. Effective managers need to ask more questions than suggest solutions in order to make the teams provide effective outcomes. An informal chat sometimes is much more effective than a formal meeting. I usually work out for 45 minutes each day and during my corporate life, I knew which of my team members liked to go for walks or exercise. I used to make it a point to talk to them for two minutes each in the morning about their exercise routine for the day. I used to take short walks with team members who I knew liked to exercise. This way I was also developing a practice to take walks along with bonding with the team members. Still, I made sure the formal corporate line was never breached; we didn't discuss work neither did we have informal conversations on video call or such. We were friendly but not friends.

Create Face Time

Even if the teams are spread across geographies and are culturally diverse, face time is important, which means being able to look eye to eye during a conversation. Managers can travel to meet the team members located in different cities/countries with the idea of generating cohesiveness and developing a rapport with them. Now, if you are dealing with teams in multiple locations like different countries or cities, frequent travelling may not be possible. In such a scenario, you may choose to have video conferences using digital tools; these meetings must be well planned and focused. Managers must ensure that the team members don't feel intimidated or nervous. Sometimes, just scheduling video conference calls for sharing humorous work stories so that the team can refresh and have some fun together. This helps in building trust within the team so that the larger purpose of a job, that is, work, is fulfilled without any conflicts or delays.

Use the Right Digital Resources

When I was being managed by bosses who were based in other locations, quite often the boss himself would not appear on the call. The times when he did attend, the skip manager working under him would be absent or very late. Eventually we used to hear things like: 'Oh, I messed up on the time zone' or 'Hey, I forgot to put it on the calendar.' Sometimes such calls were at scheduled for 6 am or 11 pm my time and waiting for the call to start at such hours of the day used to be frustrating. We are living in times when digital tools are aplenty. All managers and teammates need to do is to figure out which ones work best for them to ensure proper coordination. The tools can be segmented as:

- *Scheduling:* Doodle or Calendly.
- *Communicating:* Slack, Google Hangouts or WhatsApp (if it's a team of 4 or less).
- *Projects:* Asana and Novoed.
- *Videocon:* Zoom, GoToMeeting or Skype.
- *Virtualization:* Virbela.

IMPACT OF CULTURE IN MANAGING MULTI-LOCATIONAL GLOBAL TEAMS

While managing global projects that include team members of different ethnicities and cultures, managers face several challenges. This is because every culture has unwritten rules, which affect their thinking and actions in business situations. In some cultures, the comfort level between two parties and informal agreements are more binding than any form of formal contracts. Whereas in other work cultures that favour a professional work ethic, a detailed legal document is considered a basic requirement of operating businesses. Team members and managers often leave contextual, non-verbal cues, and read-between-the-lines messages for others to pick up on. The cohesion between managers and their team members depends a lot on how the different cultures align with one other. It is quite possible to have team members, some of whom are culturally inclined to look for meaning in a person's body language, whereas others might be attuned to precise and straight-forward words and actions. It becomes up to the managers on how effectively they pivot their own ideologies to match those of their teams so as to be able to accommodate such cultural differences, rather than employing the 'my way or the highway' approach.

To tackle diversity issues, managers can try to establish better communication pathways, guidelines and protocols to overcome the potential fallouts due to cultural differences in multi-locational teams. However, often such measures fail to yield the desired results and the team misses project deadlines, there are errors in services and generally the tension amongst the team members keeps building up. When this happens, it is advisable to approach the skip manager to figure out the undercurrent leading to performance and cohesion issues in the team and for brainstorming ideas to deal with the situation.

Managers may either be trained or read about how cultural differences can impact team collaborations so that they can avoid the pitfalls when they are managing teams that are spread globally. Culture plays a big role in the way professionals work on projects and get things done; culture affects the mindsets of people and is a part of the fundamental framework of a person's personality. Managers need to understand and accept these differences. If the manager is newly appointed, the role of the skip manager becomes critical to bring him up to speed on not just the task at hand but also the way cultural challenges need to be managed. Such contours need to be appreciated and negotiated on a daily basis when working with global teams.

Every year, a group of independent experts compiles and publishes the World Happiness Report. They rank 156 countries in the order of perceived happiness. With every working professional giving 40–80 hours at work across the world, the outcome of the survey reflects a part of the country's working culture as well. The report reveals that the citizens of Scandinavian countries such as Finland, Sweden, Denmark, Norway and Iceland are always ranked high in the happiness index. The report attributes most of this to the relaxed and employee-friendly working culture that prevails in these countries. The cultural differences are most striking when team members based in different countries get together to discuss workflows, project plans and contracts. If you send a contract document to a team that you are managing in a developed country, it's quite possible that they will detail it out and be aligned to what needs to be done to be able to meet their part of the contractual obligation. However, if the timelines and scope of work are vague, they will not be very comfortable on the course of action. Compare this to a developing country where some element of vagueness is acceptable, and the team members would expect managers to give them regular updates on what needs to be done. They would still push the envelope to deliver tasks which might have been over committed. So, the failure of a manager to provide exact details on what is needed will impact the team's morale in the US, but it might just be fine for the team in Asia. However, it's a fact that contracts need to have some leeway for revision in targets and guidelines. Hence, the managers need to ensure the teams, wherever they are, develop a mindset to not expect absolute control on circumstances and customer requirements.

Managers also face different reactions from team members in multi-locational and geographical contexts. My stint as a Vice-president at Sony Ericsson involved managing and coordinating teams in India, US, UK, Singapore and Japan. In managing projects across such diverse locations, I learnt things the hard way. The employees in the US preferred a heads-up approach when faced with potential issues in a project; the US employees never hesitated to acknowledge mistakes and relied on a collective effort to try and resolve them at the earliest. In developing economies, the experiences with diverse cultures involved more emotional considerations, where teammates were worried about saving face and were extremely sensitive to criticism. While it was never my style to be a bossy manager, the teams working in the same offices as the manager were accustomed to 'how not to disappoint the boss'; to make these team members comfortable with me, I had to direct my efforts into convincing them that 'no one is blaming you and you don't have to admit to your mistakes all the time'. The teams in Singapore and Japan had an approach to mask bad news till the time they managed to either resolve the matter at hand or were sure that the matter was out of their hands. Very seldom did they yell 'trouble' and worked to resolve problems internally. As a result of these cultural differences, there was always a need for flexibility and improvisation in my managerial approach; further, I made sure to coach the on-site managers to do the same.

Nevertheless, dealing with flexibility and improvisation was quite a challenge. When working with my counterparts in Sweden during the Ericsson assignment, the expectation was to spend a good amount of time planning the proposals and projects so that resources could be allocated in the most efficient way possible. The plans for projects had to be clearly articulated; objectives, deliverable timelines and processes had to be put on a digital tool accessible to all relevant stakeholders. It was a systematic approach, which also anticipated exigencies and showstoppers. The tool gates were the timelines at frequent intervals when milestones were to be reviewed. Few levels of managers had the authority to be able to modify the milestones and deliverables, with the objective to improvise and not completely make the project go haywire. The team's approach relied on flexibility, focusing on immediate goals of the day and everyone co-operated to ensure they were able to meet the tasks set out for the day. However, many times it was completely different as compared to the planning and approach that teams in other locations were planning to follow. It was quite a challenge to juggle between these cultural cohesions and initially, once too often, I had to approach my skip manager on the way forward. In our part of the world, this fix-it approach of taking shortcuts and not follow the process to the Tis referred to as *jugaad,* which is a more 'entrepreneurial' approach, but project management processes driven by various stakeholders in different silos.

Eventually, we were successful in the projects led by diverse, multi-locational and multicultural teams; a few things were very instrumental in making that happen.

EARLY ANTICIPATION OF TEAM'S PREFERENCE FOR WORK MANAGEMENT STYLES

There are some who are comfortable in an environment that functions on *jugaad,* preferring spontaneity and on-the-go solutions, whereas others are more comfortable with systematic and long-term planning. Having identified the persons preferring each style early on, helped bridge the gap between the two sets by developing a hybrid system of collaboration. It starts with appreciating these unique cultures: When we handed over the projects from India to Sweden, one member was designated to convert the day's work into a structured format, which was comprehensible and appreciated by the colleagues in Sweden. When the information was returned from there in the same format, one team member decoded it to help local teams understand the current status of the project. This system ensured that both teams were clear in their roles and objectives at all times. There were also sessions taken by the skip manager to address both teams collectively and individually so that all the teams understand the common goal and are on the same page. Even with time, cultural differences never automatically disappear. Therefore, managers must never turn a blind eye to such situations. It is important to view culture differences as a team's strength rather than judging them as right or wrong.

WHAT MANAGERS OF MULTI-LOCATIONAL TEAMS NEED TO LOOK OUT FOR

Often managers, who are entrusted to lead multi-locational teams if not coached properly by their skip managers during their transitioning period, can seem underconfident and nervous while handling such a team. As a result, the nervous managers see the team members leaving the company in a few months of their taking over. Sometimes even those team members who were innovative and high performing leave because of the inability of the manager to handle them. In 2019, a professional organization called Globalization Partners had conducted a survey on the intent of employees to be part of a global team. The report revealed that 72 per cent of professionals would prefer to work in multi-locational and multicultural teams. What is worth analysing is that 28 per cent of the people were not too optimistic about it. Hence, as a manager begins to see attrition, it implies that there are issues in engagement and handling, which can actually impact almost 30 per cent of the team. In such situations it is, more often than not, evident that the managers do not willingly embrace new challenges and changes brought by the different perspectives of different employees.

Where do managers go wrong? To begin with it's the element of being equally sensitive to various cultures to which the different team members belong. Due to more face time with local teams, the managers may focus more on them and make the mistake of not being able to keep morale of the whole team high. It immediately results in productivity losses. Another element where the managers go wrong is recognizing that communicating face to face and remotely on screens is not the same thing. Sometimes they don't understand how to emotionally support the distantly-located team and allay their fears, if any.

Not Appreciating Enough

Global teams are located across time zones and it's not possible for managers to know everyone personally as well as they would know the team members in the local office. Hence there are compromises whereby the managers will take a longer time to know the nature and ways of working of members in remote teams as compared to the teams working in the manager's vicinity.

Before pushing one's own agenda with the team, it's important to appreciate the team's commitment to the company and what has been achieved by them till date under the previous manager. When embracing a new global team, it's essential to start with a positive vibe by letting the teams know that you will have their back. It will keep the morale high and productivity will not suffer. The skip manager must inform the new line manager about the team members who are intrinsically motivated. In this way, the new manager can make such team members virtual coaches to encourage the ones in other locations. When teams are global and multicultural, the skips in all the locations must continue to support and second the ideas and messages of the line managers, so that the globally distanced teams don't doubt his strategies.

Causing Burnouts When Teams Are Global

Consider a team in India working in tandem with a team in Australia and Europe. With limited overlapping work hours to discuss projects, the manager has to rely on giving a significant autonomy to the globally spread teams. However, certain behavioural aspects of managers like making teams work extended hours, on weekends and keep pushing for near impossible timelines, causes the team members to burnout by being overworked. One reason for this is the new line manager emulating the skip manager's organizational style of pushing the envelope hard, thinking it best that the practice continues. The other reason is that managers get tempted to work the best people harder than others and that sets the trap for frequent attritions. Managers don't realize that high performing, overworked employees tend to think they are being punished for being productive and effective in delivering great performance. Research conducted by Stanford University showed that productivity per hour declines sharply when employees are pushed to work more than 50 hours a week. In India, working 12 hours a day, 70–80 hours a week is a norm in some industries. However, a manager handling teams in Asia and Europe, might be tempted to impose similar hours there as well; the result would be to fail miserably. Managers must be able to give a higher workload to talented employees, but not so much so that they feel suffocated to such a level that they exit. Especially in the Indian context, working weekends seems to be a given, but try pushing this on teams in other parts of the world and a manager might be facing very stiff resistance. If managers keep increasing the workload because people initially accept it, then the global teams would either collectively complain or high performers will exit.

Show-Stopping

Ever heard about managers who won't let someone rise up the ranks and sacrifice their upward mobility, to further their own interests? In a global framework, the competition to grow and look at better internal opportunities is fiercer. Today, every company has Internal Job Posts (IJP); however, some managers obstruct members of their teams, applying to internal roles, for the fear of losing talent. While in certain cultures the employees won't go against the manager, but in many economies the employee will directly go and complain about the manager show stopping his growth. If the teams tend to believe that the manager is not going to move them up the ladder in their career, the team members feel let down and start lacking the enthusiasm to deliver with their full potential. Opportunities for advancement being kept out of reach by managers is a serious morale killer. For three years in my career, I was not able to move to better jobs through IJPs because my boss didn't want my services to be rendered to another department. While being the favourite of my immediate superior had its own perks, it was stunting my professional growth. Eventually I approached my skip manager to let him know how I was feeling. However, the skip dismissed it as a problem between me and my manager; I waited a couple of months and eventually resigned. It was not out of frustration, but the realization that my manager was overly dependent on me, so much so that it was holding me back from growing as a professional.

When blessed with a talented global team, it's the manager's responsibility to present them with avenues for expanding their skill set and enhance their careers.

The Blamer Approach

Managers dealing with cross functional and multi-locational teams have a deeper tendency to not admit their mistakes or oversights. It stems from the fear of being questioned and challenged by people from other countries. Such managers create a culture full of fear and anxiety where the inactions of a manager are blamed on lack of follow-ups from the team. The issue especially arises when a manager shrugs off responsibility for his actions to avoid being humiliated in front of team members from various nationalities. Managers who are bravely leading global teams should consider themselves equally accountable for actions that show both results and the lack thereof. Managers that keep blaming their teams for non-performance also follow-up such conversations with a threat to fire them from the job. When there are multi-locational and multicultural teams involved, the manager cannot isolate an individual to blame for shortfall and hence the personal threats of termination are reduced. If the teams are local, the manager would know the people much better to know their pressure points and hence might continue to pose termination threats. The managers shouldn't create such a toxic work environment; sooner or later employees take to escalating the issue or find other jobs.

Lisa Sabilia: Impact Leader and Professional Artist

Lisa is a Co-CEO of Youtopian and a change leader based out of the east coast of USA.

Intentionally leaping towards addressing my greatest weakness required self-management and instinctual curiosity to accelerate learning potential. She believes that being a manager to lead the teams comes regardless of the location where a person is based or the situation the person is in.

Action and integrity are cornerstones of management. She pushes the parameters of improvement through change agents and supports those around her regardless of the hierarchy status.

The people that you deal with as managers or colleagues across nations and cultures can grow together through collaboration and collective wisdom which can lead to pioneering of new-age best practices as outcomes. Transformative management is a bridge of authentic values that evolves through lessons from the past, both for the managers as well as the team members in multiple locations. Pinnacle leaders propel forward through instinct, ambition, reason and curiosity. Integrated teams across cultures are driven by a common purpose and are not limited by respective roles. Their speed of progress is fuelled by the intrinsic will to overachieve expectations and collaborate with people around.

Seeing the Big Picture

If managers supervising multicultural and multi-location teams want their best people to stay with them and deliver, then treating them equally must be thought through carefully. Often managers are not willing to embrace a multicultural and multi-locational workforce, since they are not certain of the efforts being put by everyone in the team. To negate this belief, managers set up clear guidelines and escalation matrices. In one of my earlier assignments, the customer issues were labelled as Critical, Important and Manageable to assign them due levels of priority. For the critical issues, the team had to attend resolution meetings irrespective of time zones; for important issues, they were asked by the manager to attend; and the manageable issues were resolved during office hours only. This way all the teammates in multiple geographies had a buy-in. Alongside, we had no restriction on when to write and email since others can read when they want. At times, matters of importance were emailed to employees in other time zones; if any of the employees were able to initiate action immediately, they did so. This way, devoting time to official work after hours was a voluntary choice and not enforced by the manager.

Managers, who are to supervise global teams for the first time, find it difficult to ascertain how to best introduce their mandates. Meanwhile, those who have already got their hands in the global waters continue improving on the practices already established by them. There were no restrictions on emailing to anyone at any time since it was an open culture and people could read emails as per their availability and working hours. Attitudes and beliefs impact how managers can motivate others. Pushing teams to work on something is not as good as making them believe that the work they are doing is important. When the team understands the importance of a specific goal, they need to be trusted to deliver on expectations. Overall, adoption of technology led routines cannot replace the need for development of trust, transparency and responsibility between people who need to work as teams. It is important to get to know team members personally and treat them as individuals as much as a collective group responsible for delivering on a task; it is also important to be aware of cultural differences so that it doesn't conflict with priorities. If a manager schedules a project patch delivery on a day one of the team members in another part of the word has to celebrate his child's first birthday, a compromise is written on the wall. Further, it is relevant to focus on outcomes rather than the hours one clocks; this will allow flexibility to employees to work out the most productive and cooperative framework.

SKIP LEVELS AND LARGE TEAMS MANAGEMENT IN 'FLAT' ORGANIZATIONS

Lately, it seems everyone is talking about an interconnected world with flat and collaborative culture instead of hierarchical organizations. In an ideal situation, a flat organization would be able to leverage talent, passion and experience of every employee, irrespective of hierarchy, and encourage and harness their individual potentials to solve business challenges. The difference between a contemporary and traditional structure in organizations is that a contemporary flat structure blurs the line dividing the teams, subordinate managers and skip managers. It implies that a flat organization promotes an increased involvement of all levels in decision-making with less supervision and more autonomy. With more levels, the requirements and opinions of people keep adding to costs and put a dent in the budget. In effect if the employees, at all levels, are not agile in decision-making, it might lead to loss of time and hence opportunities. However, even if one or two, a hierarchy in the organization is still a hierarchy. If there are hierarchies, the skip management levels functionally develop by default. While implementing a flat organization structure, there are also chances of increasing confusion as to the role of different employees and credit sharing. Since everyone is potentially able to talk to everyone in a flat organization, there can be frequent and unnecessary escalations that can take a toll on the work to be done. It's possible that a mid-sized organization with up to 100 employees can implement a flat structure more effectively. However, as companies grow in size and scale and spread over geographies, the need for levels and delegation increases many-fold.

While flat organizations are able to reduce the time to decision-making and in effect the implementation of plans, as they grow the levels increase. At this time, the companies need to ensure that with increase in the number of employees and hierarchies, the information experience doesn't get distorted and the transparency in decision-making still remains intact. As the organizations grow, many of them don't manage to remain flat and hence the hierarchical levels begin to increase. As the hierarchies come into play when flat organizations grow, the employees start to feel the gap between them and senior levels. These employees are used to direct communication with all levels and such a change in organization structure might lead to many deciding to leave the company, increasing attrition.

Flat organizations need to create a fine balance between the time taken in decision-making and the precision that's needed to get the work done. In flat organizations, employees might feel empowered since they can escalate any issue to any level, wasting the management's time in matters that don't need their executive attention. Since the employees' communication with senior management is transparent, the middle management can feel disappointed and out of place at times.

LEARNING FROM THE INDUSTRY LEADERS

Below is an interview with Mr Lloyd Mathias, who is a pan-Asia business leader, marketeer and strategist with intimate knowledge of the region and a proven track record of creating compelling visions and driving business performance across the consumer, telecom and technology domains. He has led and motivated teams on a platform of trust, performance and respect. Lloyd has run profit and loss accounts and driven positive commercial outcomes in global companies—HP, Tata, Motorola and PepsiCo.

Question 1: What are the challenges faced by individual contributors transitioning into FTMs and skip managers?

The only thing to be learned is how to lead and manage a team. So, the individual contributor has to learn to handle people and recognize that people will need clear objectives, motivation, leadership and continuous communication. A big element the new IC has to cultivate is empathy. He now has to take into account that his team member needs to feel appreciated and see him as someone who he can reach out to help him solve his problems.

Skip managers should make sure to not go directly to the IC but keep the reporting manager in the loop. As a skip manager, it is also important for him to keep a close eye on the dynamics of his reporting manager and the ICs he works with.

Question 2: How can skip managers make or break the organization culture?

The skip managers typically help translate the organization culture of collaboration, creation, competition from senior management to frontline and individual contributors. They need to balance operational management (tasks) with people management (empathy). They also need to be sensitive to the ICs and ensure that the teams' concerns are properly conveyed to, and resolved, with the senior management.

Question 3: What are the dos and don'ts when thinking about jumping over the boss's head?

In general, it is best to avoid. However, there may be situations when there is a compelling need to go the skip level—when it is important to state the context to the skip manager. Also, find a reasonable way to communicate whatever has been discussed with the skip to the reporting manager so that he doesn't feel completely out of the loop. Not doing so will lay the groundwork for the likelihood of a strained relationship, laced with mistrust, between the IC and his/her immediate manager.

Question 4: What are the issues that arise when multi-locational/multicultural teams are to be handled? How to minimize miscommunication and mitigate the challenges?

When managing multi-locational and multicultural teams, first and foremost it is important to set and communicate a clear cadence. Set up a bi-weekly call or a weekly staff meeting (remote) with a clear agenda to each of these calls. It is equally important to plan for a physical team meeting so that everyone gets the chance to build the necessary bonds and personal equations—this should also be on a set basis, ideally quarterly.

Always keep cultural sensitivities in mind; publicly reprimanding erring employees may not go down well with certain cultures. Stay sensitive to this. Also, as far as possible, follow up on key oral announcements with a written communication. Be very sensitive to time zones and peoples work hours.

Question 5: What are the challenges faced by managers when the team grows in number?

The main challenge is setting clear objectives and being able to give every team member enough time and attention. Many companies follow a span of control of 7-10 as optimal, which means that a manager will not have more than 10 people reporting into him/her. However, irrespective of the number, it is important to budget for one-on-one time with each team member, even if it is a 10-minute call or face-to-face meeting. Not all issues come up in a team meeting.

The other challenge is recognizing and addressing intra-team issues; disagreements and clashes between team members can mar a team's overall performance.

Question 6: How strong are executive isolation dynamics in organizations and why? Why do managers try to keep their bosses isolated from the teams?

Typically, insecure managers fear their bosses' interaction with their reportees. This happens because they feel their team members may—with a view to impress the skip-level boss—talk about certain performance or behavioural issues of the manager which they would like to report to the skip levels. Further, a deep-rooted fear that the team member may complain about the manager's management style or ineffectiveness in supervising the team, contributes to the isolation tactics.

Question 7: What is the impact of managers getting friendly with reportees and then not being able to detach themselves from the reportees after becoming skip managers? How can confusion caused by parallel authorities be avoided?

This is a real problem given the weakening of hierarchies. It tends to get difficult if a newly promoted manager doesn't let go of his earlier team despite having a larger team to manage. This may tend to alienate the new members of his team.

As such, a newly elevated manager must go out of his way to ensure his new team feels that he is as concerned about then as the team he previously directly managed; he may ensure this by spending a disproportionate amount of time with them in the initial period of his leadership.

Question 8: Whether leaders should always take charge of business strategies and/or solutions or display the ability to question, listen and learn from their teams?

The best way leadership teams can create better managers is by focusing on a meritocratic culture, strategy and ethics and empowering the operational managers' executive actions. Moreover, it is important for an organizations' leadership to have an ear on the ground reality—both to hear from its customers and the front-line employees. The more the organization moulds it's approach basis the customers' needs, the better will the execution be.

FURTHER READINGS

Bloom, Nicholas, James Liang, John Roberts, and Zhichun Jenny Ying. 2015. 'Does Working from Home Work? Evidence from a Chinese Experiment.' https://nbloom.people.stanford.edu/sites/g/files/sbiybj4746/f/wfh.pdf

Gestner, Louis. 2002. *Who Says Elephants Can't Dance?* New York: HarperCollins.

'Globalization Partners Report.' https://www.globalization-partners.com/about-us/company-news/globalization-partners-and-shrm-report-companies-struggle-to-manage-global-teams/

Society for Human Resource Management. 2017. '2017 Employee Benefits: Remaining Competitive in a Challenging Talent Marketplace.' https://www.shrm.org/hr-today/trends-and-forecasting/research-and-surveys/pages/2017-employee-benefits.aspx#:~:text=Nearly%20one%2Dthird%20of%20organizations,may%20now%20be%20leveling%20off

Welch, Jack. 2001. *Straight from the Gut.* New York: Warner Books.

'World Happiness Report.' https://worldhappiness.report/archive/

DYNAMICS BETWEEN MANAGERIAL LEVELS: THE DOS AND DON'TS!

Managers at all levels face certain challenges on how to avoid their teams feeling awkward or self-conscious, what would the managers need to give up between authority and influence in order to manage the teams effectively, how not to make team members feel alone, help teams embrace change and how to provide the required resources for teams to perform effectively. For instance, team members may feel left out that leads them to perceive the manager's nonchalance as lack of support. It's a daily happening that reportees approach their bosses, with a spark in their eyes, to discuss a new idea or an innovative tweak to an old process but get turned down by the bosses. The reportee may have thought that his idea was unique, got excited about it and believed that the manager will appreciate his going out of the traditional way and be happy about the team thinking out of the box. However, what should one do when the boss says 'no' to something you were very passionate about?

At the outset, it is always better to first negotiate with your immediate manager to discuss an idea. Good managers do not dismiss their reportees without providing a rationale for rejecting their ideas; instead they make it a point to tell their reportees why an idea, presumably good, is not the right one to implement at a given time; successful managers ensure they appreciate the team member for making an effort. However, more often than not, the reportee feels dejected and acting on a humanly impulse, jumps ship to get his ideas heard by the higher-ups in the organization.

From a manager's perspective, it is frustrating when a reportee goes over their head to approach the skip manager. A manager, naturally, feels left out of discussions and tends to believe the worst, that the reportee is trying to make him look bad in front of the skip manager.

SACHIO'S EXPERIENCES

Sachio Nishioka is a Stanford LEAD alumnus, a former MD of MUFG Bank in Japan and currently the general manager of Mitsubishi UFJ Research & Consulting.

Sachio recounts his experiences from his previous place of work. He started by telling me about a skip manager, who had a strong expertise in global business management and a middle manager, who was an expert in domestic business management but no experience in global business management. Their team handled a plethora of clients; as such, they were involved in a mix of global business and domestic business management. At times, the person in charge (the client manager) would be faced with the need to discuss issues pertaining to global businesses. In such cases, the client manager, in light of the skip manager's expertise in the subject, took a call to directly approach him, knowing that the immediate manager might not be able to give the right guidance. The client manager made sure to keep the middle manager in the loop while emailing the skip manager for a meeting request ensuring that the middle manager is aware that he is jumping the queue to discuss a matter with the skip manager in which the skip manager is an expert; thus, ensuring the middle manager does not feel insecure. The skip manager would reply to the client manager's email by keeping the middle manager in the mail thread, following the company's protocol to maintain transparency. Similarly, the team also got cases requiring the middle manager's expertise in local business management. In such situations, the skip manager made sure to discuss the client's business with the middle manager. Both of them seems to respect each other however the client manager seems to lose respect for his immediate manager for overall strategic line of sight to business.

According to Sachio, if a skip manager decides to take initiative on some projects, which are in the domain of the middle manager, it should be limited to when it is crucial for the organization that a person in the higher management should take charge; however, this should be an exception rather than a practice. Also, the skip should insist that the meetings are attended by the middle manager; this would help avoid team members trying to directly approach the skip managers without intimating the immediate managers. This would avoid the tendency of reportees to jump the immediate manager's head and go directly to the skip. This kind of level hopping, if it happens often, can be detrimental to the repute and respect due to the middle manager. If the middle manager is unable to attend the meetings, it is prudent that the skip manager shares the minutes and actions taken in the meeting with the middle manager, so that the tactical execution is managed by the staff with the middle manager. Level hopping is a time saviour when it comes to strategic decision-making, however, a lack of information sharing can complete throw the manager-team relationship out of equation.

WHAT CAN CAUSE RIFTS BETWEEN MANAGERIAL LEVELS?

Imagine a situation at the workplace when an employee believes that his idea can solve a problem. On approaching the manager, he gets a firm 'no' and no opportunity for discussion at all. What should one do when the manager declines any ideas that come from the team members? A situation may arise when a reportee has a great idea to resolve a business emergency that needs a quick response, but the manager isn't on board. Should the person go over the manager's head? When is it okay to jump levels and take your ideas to the skip manager or to an even higher-up in the management chain? If you do figure out when, how do you approach the senior manager? Would jumping levels impact your career for the better or worse? These questions trouble independent contributors very often in their careers.

The problem between managerial levels can develop at various instances. The forthcoming section discusses some of these instances.

The first level is when a colleague goes to his manager with an idea or suggestion and comes back disappointed. He needs to decide whether to approach the same manager again or take his proposal to a skip manager. The manager might not be able to hear his team members out due to lack of time and work pressure; or he may not be able to see the big picture that the team member wants to show him. The skip manager, on the other hand, would probably dismiss anyone from two levels down coming and present an idea which his immediate manager has already decided to ignore. These functional interplays between managerial levels don't have a direct construct when someone tries to jump over the manager's head. However, the onus is on the skip manager to enforce escalation protocols in case someone tries to reach out to them over the immediate manager's head. These functional dimensions don't have a direct answer, but the ones seem to be on the skip manager to ensure the protocols are in order, if someone tries to reach out over the manager's head.

Another situation that may cause a rift between managerial levels is when a manager is transferred to a new division and his or her reportees want to unsettle him. This is possible when the reportees still have easy access to their previous manager who is at a level above the transferee manager.

Renny was a professional with 10 years of experience and was given a promotion from a senior product expert to marketing manager. Her boss was of the opinion that Renny had the potential to be a diversified manager and hence was moved to a new division as an FTM. She took charge of a division with four employees reporting to her in the marketing analysis division. What Renny didn't realize was that there was a team member, Jake, who was upset about not having been promoted to the position that Renny now held. Jake started going over Renny's head to feed false information to her manager about her lack of managerial capabilities and how she was not up to speed on what was expected from the team. Jake was able to do this because he had previously worked with Renny's manager for a few years and was in good terms with him. Renny had no clue that this was happening; she had no way of knowing that her own reportee was going over her head, due to a preconceived notion of being more deserving.

Renny's manager trusted Jake's information on face value and began questioning her abilities to lead the department. So, one day Renny got a call from her manager who asked her why she was not treating everyone in the team equally. He told her that certain members of her team were feeling overlooked despite their capabilities. Renny was taken aback by the accusation. When asked about the source of this information, her manager was professional enough to tell her that he was receiving such inputs from Jake.

Renny kept calm and handled things right. She did not lose her composure and refuted the claims without getting edgy or defensive. Secondly, she appreciated her manager's transparency in revealing the source of the allegations, indicating that he had no personal vendetta in blaming her. Lastly, Renny informed her manager that she would speak to Jake in person to figure out his concerns. The manager agreed to her plan and despite her being an FTM, he trusted her plan of action.

She discussed the matter with Jake, who offered no explanation. The lesson Renny learnt from this episode was to ensure the need of a stronger relationship with her boss. Renny started to have a 'weekly updates' discussion with her boss, which he also welcomed. She openly sought guidance about management of team dynamics and asked him if he had got any other feedback about her. Renny made it clear to Jake that she was speaking with her boss every week and all business and team matters were being openly discussed. Jake never went over her head again, realizing that Renny's manager trusted her. However, since Jake kept demonstrating resistance to align, his performance started suffering. Having no other option, Renny, for the benefit of both, the team and Jake, requested her manager to find a new role for Jake to suit his skills and ambitions. Renny continued her good work; the team also realized that she had earned her manager's trust. For the next decade, Renny had got promoted thrice and her team continued to excel under her leadership. Her stint as manager went well for her since she did not succumb to alarm and anxiety when her team went over her head; instead she handled the matter patiently and honestly.

TO LEAVE OR NOT TO LEAVE, THAT IS THE URGE

People don't just leave due to immediate managers.

There is a cliché that people don't leave companies, they leave managers. But have we ever thought about which manager are they leaving—the reporting manager or a skip manager? It is true that sometimes people resign because they don't get along with their manager; but that manager need not necessarily be the reporting manager. Second- or third-level skips have a much significant impact when it comes to employee engagement, retention and attrition—an element that's little analysed during exit interviews. The employee mostly doesn't even get a chance to talk about an issue he may have had with a certain higher-up in the company majorly because the HR doesn't ask the right questions.

In their careers many professionals leave jobs due to immediate managers and take jobs elsewhere due to the credentials of the skip and higher-level managers. However once in an organization, everyone needs to balance between just obeying the boss and the temptation to go over his head.

Should you control that urge? When it's a matter of the manager saying no to your requirement, idea or expectation, it's good to try again a few times to keep negotiating for a buy in. It is better to not be hasty about jumping the queue. If the manager is declining your requests and mandates, it's critical to find out why. However, if you decide to go over the manager's head, it should not be done stealthily. Yet, it's seldom the case that professionals gather the courage to tell their managers of their plan to go over to the skip. If you tell the manager, he may be supportive, or he could be indifferent, or he could be offended. But if you go to the skip without your manager's knowledge, he will most definitely be offended and could even possibly get back at you in some way.

In most situations corporate leaders believe that trying to go over the boss is not a good policy; it needs to be an exception and not a practice. One must not go around the manager just because the manager is not able to conduct meetings effectively or isn't buying-in to the team's ideas. Jumping over the manager's head is not just challenging but can turn out to be risky as well. An employee who tends to alienate a manager gets the same treatment in return resulting in a breakdown of mutual ownership. The experienced suggest that one can always approach other people at the same level as the manager for advice. However, one can always wait for a formal gathering where both skips and reporting managers are present, to discuss any issues with the skip managers without any risk of offending the reporting manager, since, technically, you are not going over the manager's head.

However, there are certain situations that warrant going over the manager's head; the general position is if the situation involves harassment, unethical/immoral practices or illegal work, reporting the same to the higher management is acceptable and even encouraged. Texas Instrument's (TI) former CEO Brian Crutcher was ousted within seven weeks of being CEO for undisclosed behaviour ethics issues, even though he worked for the company for 22 years. If the person believes that the matter at hand requires action against any unethical practices, then the unethical practices should be reported to the higher management. Employees indicate a strong preference for corporates that are respected for their ethics. Hence, employer branding takes centre stage in such cases. However, in cases of managers being abusive, disrespectful or harassing, there is a protocol for reporting such behaviour. I was once is such a situation. My manager used to keep me in office till 2–3 AM almost every day under the pretext of 'urgent work'. After a few months I realized that the work could have been done at a comfortable pace; it was just the manager's pattern to make employees spend extra hours at work for no reason. Eventually, one day, I went ahead and told him that I have zero tolerance for this kind of behaviour and I strongly felt the need to inform HR about the manager keeping me at work for more than 15 hours every day without a valid reason. However, I had to exercise caution since this manager had been in the company for more than a decade and everyone knew about his irrational need to keep people in office for long hours. Still the manager was flourishing and going strong. It's quite tempting to go over the manager's head when you are superseded by someone else for a promotion or you want support from senior quadrants. However, if not planned and executed well, going over your manager can turn out to be risky and isolating. It is better to have a mental checklist to decide whether a situation demands a necessary jump over the manager's head, or the situation may be resolved without going over the manager's head. It is better to avoid skipping if it can be avoided. All of us working in corporates report to someone or the other. If an employee is lucky, they get a boss who knows what the right thing to do would be; eventually such managers become mentors to their subordinates.

When you have the urge to skip over your boss's head, please understand that managers are human too; they make mistakes and don't always have the right answers. There are situations where one can clearly visualize major business losses, but the manager is too caught up in other work to act. However, the team members may not want to be in the side-lines and would like to address the loss by first talking to the manager. If that does not work, they may consider going over the manager's head to approach the next managerial level.

It's seldom you get to work with the desired boss, so it is best to accept that whether ridiculously under-qualified or a rock star, he is first your supervisor, and someone made him your boss for a reason. Further, the first thing a boss expects from the subordinates is respect. So, if you are seriously considering going over your manager's head, here are some checkpoints to be considered for a rationale decision.

WHEN NOT TO GO OVER THE BOSS'S HEAD

At some point or another, during one's career, he or she tends to think the worst about their job as well as their manager. However, as much as one may like to think that their boss is the devil incarnate, the reason for such unpleasant feelings may not be the boss. For example, if your boss continues to give you routine and monotonous assignments, even though, in the appraisal you expressed a desire for more strategy based responsibilities, there must be a reason—he is probably assigning petty jobs to qualified staff because of paucity of strategy roles and to ensure that the staff does not come under the cost-cutting scanner because of such paucity. This situation should first entitle the person to talk to the immediate manager. In case the responses are not satisfactory, one may consider jumping over the boss's head and talk about the situation to the skip manager/s.

In one of my VP level assignments, there was an employee who complained whenever I assigned a task to him. This had been recurring for about six months and since I had not been a part of the company for long, I tried to find ways of reengaging him, but there was no change in the person's attitude. Eventually, I asked him for a one-on-one meeting to sort out the matter and he said that the profile dissatisfaction was a direct result of my management style and my lack of understanding of the background of the company business since I came from an unrelated sector. Post our conversation, I spent some time introspection. In the mean while the employee had already gone to my manager and expressed his frustration to him.

Not surprisingly, I had a visit from my manager the very same day; At first, he kept things light, asking me about how the last few months had been for me as we walked from the pantry to his cabin. However, once we settled in his room, my manager didn't waste any more time to inform me of the frustration that my team member had expressed to him. I was kind of devastated to hear that despite our meeting, barely a few hours ago, this person chose to jump the level instead of trying to figure out a way of working together. This discussion with my manager was quite a blow to my confidence and despite being able to maintain professional decorum, I was personally hurt. My manager didn't offer any advice since he wanted me to figure out a way ahead on my own. In retrospect, I realized that was quite a mature and professional gesture. For the next few weeks, I began to self-doubt my management style, just because one member of the team had jumped levels. I couldn't help thinking, why this was such a big deal to me; why was the loyalty of one employee so important?

Over a period of next few months, I focused on delivering key performance indicators (KPIs) more than getting upset with one employee's behaviour. Eventually, one day he came around and said, 'I think it's not you, I generally don't like my job. Maybe I should have kept discussing with you on how to make the job more satisfying rather than going and talk to your manager.' He had a self-realization that I, as his manager, was not the issue, the work itself had got to him. That was when I realized it wasn't so much as disloyalty of one employee that affected me; it was the fact that there wasn't anything I had done to him on a personal or professional level that could warrant such an attitude. Eventually he applied for an internal job posting in a unit handling new products; sometimes we caught up to talk about his work. However, he spent a few months working on the new assignment to handover the assignment to his successor and we remained cordial professional acquaintances.

WHEN YOU MUST GO OVER THE BOSS'S HEAD

One does not need to play the role of a whistle-blower and get a company's corporate governance and ethics division involved every time they see something amiss. However, if you see something consistently out of place and your manager is central or peripheral to the thing that is out of place, then you should report such amiss behaviour. The saying, 'If you see something, say something,' made famous by the US Department of Homeland Security, is applicable even in the professional arena. Corporate governance training is essential for all employees and should be done at regular intervals. However, very few organizations make it happen and hence employees themselves start making judgment calls if they feel there is a breach of the code of conduct.

I've have had the misfortune of reporting to an abusive boss. After months of suffering at his hands, I gathered the courage to not follow his orders. It was a very nervous moment for me and a tricky one indeed, since the circumstances were delicate and no one else seemed to mind my manager's behaviour. Simply running to his boss's cabin and giving an emotional pitch about my manager's behaviour was not going to work out. Instead, I kept taking note of instances of abusive behaviour projected by my manager on different members of the team, including me, and how that impacted the team's morale that led to the slippage in adhering to project timelines. I kept a tab on the names of people abused, on what days and in which meetings; I even jotted down what was being discussed in the meetings when the manager went berserk. When I could not handle his unacceptable behaviour any longer, I approached two managers at higher levels to discuss my experience. During the conversation I expressed concern for myself, the team, the company and the boss. What was of importance was to approach the right person who will appreciate that my complaint is in the best interest of the company and not a vindictive act against the manager. The skip levels acted with pragmatism and ensured the anonymity of our conversations.

Don't: When You're Trying to Bypass the Manager for Promotions

In every organization, you find people who are on a lookout for opportunities of side-lining the boss to take his place. It is quite a mistake to plan such a manoeuvre. As managers analyse areas of improvement in team members, the reportees are also on a lookout for the boss's weaknesses. During meetings where higher management is also in attendance, such employees start to position themselves ahead of the manager and in an ingenious manner, subtly try to discredit the boss. In such situations, smart bosses identify such employees as opportunists, not ambitious. Before they realize, such employees are grounded and overlooked during the promotions and increments cycle. Managers look for collaboration and ability to be team players in their reportees. How an employee responds to a manager's stimulus and that of the skip levels, can be a direct reflection of what lies ahead for him.

Do: If You Are Facing Hostility and Harassment

Harassment and hostility are very subjective issues when it comes to deciding whether to jump the level or not. It seems quite obvious that one should go to the skip levels if they are facing hostility and harassment from their reporting managers, however, what is hostile for one person may not be hostile for another, thereby making it a 'not so straightforward' decision.

That is why every employee must insist to know the anti-hostility and anti-harassment policy of the company.

I have heard colleagues talk about their experiences of undergoing harassment in some job or another. As per them, the harassment and intolerance ranged from sexist comments to delayed increments. Most of them didn't do a thing for years of undergoing such troublesome times and that has been their biggest regret till date. If a manager has suffered harassment and hostility in his own career, he may end up taking it out on his own team and make them suffer such humiliation. Such situations make a true case for going over the manager's head.

It is very difficult to tell a skip manager that the manager he promoted under him to lead the team doesn't have the ability to do so. It feels impossible to let the higher levels know that manager/s below them harass some employees and behave in a hostile manner with a few. One never knows if the skip level knows it already and chooses to turn a blind eye as long as the impugned manager is delivering results. Another reason for employees undergoing harassment or bearing the brunt of their reporting managers hostile behaviour to not take their complaints to the higher levels may be an apprehension that he or she will be seen as an opportunist.

Jumping over the boss's head needs courage, however, if done professionally through facts and data, the matter can be addressed and resolved amicably and quickly. If a manager is asking the team to not take company policies and code of conducts seriously, then the team members should report such matters to higher authorities with a clear account of each instance when their manager asked them to overlook company policies. Just like such episodes where a manager is making teammates uncomfortable, if the boss is asking the team to not practice company policies or ethics, one must gather as much details as possible and bring it to the notice of higher levels. This situation warrants a jump over the boss's head. Every employee has the right to work in a safe, secure, ethical and professionally conducive environment. It's the job of a manager to assure such conditions prevail at work.

An employee who has the courage to report wrongdoings at any levels, even if it means jumping over the manager's head, is well poised to become a future leader. The organization sees his/her ability to adhere to ethics, capability of critical thinking and effective decision-making and not be intimidated.

LEADERSHIP CRISIS ACROSS VARIOUS LEVELS

According to a Gallup poll of 2016, only 18 per cent of managers in the US demonstrated high level of ability to manage others, which implies that 82 per cent of the proclaimed managers didn't have the ability to manage people. It also implies that the teams reporting to the 82 per cent of sub-optimal managers could be looking at a career development that is bad for their professional futures. Lack of leadership abilities across levels not only puts the organizations at risk but also the high-potential individuals who get caught in the crossfires between managers who are clueless about directions and strategies.

Employees are quick to figure out the kind of manager they are dealing with. A good one shapes teams that are trustworthy and the bad one is left with people who are working out of fear or compulsion. Organizations appraise people on the basis of their past performances with little emphasis on their skills; demonstrating that ambition and competitiveness is rewarded. The inflated sense of being indispensable to the company and the perception of 'power' corrupts managers irrespective of the levels they are at. Rising up the ranks, many managers become abusive and deaf to the team's voices. This can lead to a climate of intimidation. Such an environment becomes conducive to people deciding to exit the organization or go over the reporting manager's head to make their voices heard in front of the higher-ups of the company. Being a skip manager, in conditions where the teams below are dealing with a trying middle manager, can be very difficult. As one starts to feel powerful and 'in control', empathy starts to take a back seat.

MASSIMO: SKIP MANAGERS NEED TO BE IN A MEDITATIVE STATE

Massimo is a Stanford alumnus, a corporate digital innovation executive turned social entrepreneur and the founder of AlterContacts.

Massimo aspires to help people, organizations, companies, cities and countries to be smarter, to explore different options for solving problems and to understand the full implications of their decisions; in short, to think before they act. He has braved the corporate world for close to three decades and experienced multi-level management from close quarters. Here is what Massimo has to say about the dynamics of managerial levels.

'So...you are a skip manager!'—the face of his HR BP showed she had just found a rare breed, or at least a profile she did not encounter often.

Massimo learnt to be a manager in the American manufacturing world where one can talk directly to anyone anytime, and he became used to the progressive culture in companies like IBM, where hierarchy was irrelevant as long as every person, irrespective of his stature in the company, contributed to achieve and exceed targets and delivering targets. Subsequently, his years in the maritime hospitality industry also contributed to developing his collaborative skills; working in large teams; and managing multi-level engagements. True enough, on board the cruise ships, the hierarchy was strictly imposed and adhered to; the dedication and discipline required on board the ship were as close to resembling the military since survival was of paramount importance, still the priority was to satisfy and, if possible, to exceed customer expectations. The high-level priority ensured that peers collaborated within the assigned boundaries of responsibilities, and every officer on board intervened or took leadership of a situation if needed, even if the people involved were not part of his or her department. It's a true demonstration of multi-level and multicultural collaboration, teamwork and people management.

To give a simple example, when Massimo was in charge of the IT department for the high-power division of Power-One (now ABB), he was leading a team that was responsible for the factories that built power suppliers for the internet. Their main customers were a bunch of fortune 500 companies including CISCO, HP and Teradyne. From the factories, power was being supplied every twelve seconds, in a 24x7 operation. If you tell the logistics team that they had to 'open a ticket' in case a bar code printer stopped working, what kind of response do you expect? Massimo recalls that during the end of the financial quarter, if there was a delay or last-minute emergency, the VP of Operations himself would get down to the manufacturing floor, help package boxes and drive the forklift. That was a great example of commitment to results and an indication of adaptability between the manager and the team members.

What was Massimo's experience when he first started working in that company? He recalls entering the factories from the shipping docks; checking on the logistics crew to make sure their day started without any roadblocks; then walking his way through packaging, testing, manual assembly lines and robotized machines. By the time he reached office, and before meeting his peers, Massimo already took care of dispatching the crew to fix anything that may threaten the smooth operation of the factory. His peers and superiors were happy that Massimo took care of his team and others, because under his leadership everyone was doing a better job together.

The impact of this way of management, when it gets supported and rewarded by the higher-ups, is contagious—Massimo's team members began to imitate his compassion, empathy and razor-sharp focus in meeting customer commitments. Everyone was extremely busy preventing disasters from happening, but also extremely satisfied with the results, and so was Massimo's boss and the boss's boss. The team functioned without resorting to blame games; as such, there was no distress. The team worked like a well-oiled machine, meeting expectations and sometimes exceeding them.

Massimo's experience in Carnival Corporation was also similar; to make sure the ship was running as smooth as a swiss clock, Massimo would make sure to visit each department every day, to keep himself aware of any possible and probable issues the team might face and prevent them from happening in the first place, instead of fire-fighting.

Coming back to work in Europe for the first time, he took a job in the Netherlands, a country that is famous for an advanced work culture. This was a large multinational company and Massimo expected the same culture and job description as was advertised on the career tab on their website. He arrived with a lot of energy and ambition to deliver results and brought in the political posture of 'open workplace' for promoting collaboration and creativity.

After a glorious career across continents and companies to manage people and businesses, it was surprising that he ended up being coached by HR for presumably 'jumping the levels'.

What Happened: The Situation

The matter was quite simple. In order to understand the big picture and other contemporary organizational dynamics, Massimo had to use a design thinking approach and observe the ways of working of 100+ executives across three organizations. He looked at what they do and how they do it, to discover why they act in a certain way. After an extensive empathy mapping exercise, it all became clear: He found that the only thing executives, directors and managers in Europe are interested in, was to protect their personal image and reputation. Everything else, including the future of the company, was deemed irrelevant by majority of the company's population.

Moreover, he discovered that the educational system in northern Europe had been shifting from providing knowledge to training the students to display a particular type of behaviour. In the Netherlands there are schools, even universities, that advertise 'teaching to speak as...'—fill in the space with the highest level one can reach in a particular profession—in their curriculum presentations. That is part of the value proposition for the candidate student. Gaining knowledge is played down and scientists are considered to be at a lower level than the management. A scientist in the Netherlands makes less money than a project manager. Managers avoid doing anything that portrays them as 'functional' (the Dutch use that word in an almost deceptive way when referring to professionals).

A contributing factor for this is that companies in Europe are run and controlled by the finance team, and not by marketing or operations, like in most other countries including the US. The companies talk a lot about market and customer centricity, which actually remain only words since the companies don't practice them: They don't 'Walk the Talk'. Every employee, irrespective of executive or managerial levels, knows the gap between the talk and practices but no one talks about it openly in order to not put their careers in jeopardy. And we all know it, we just cannot say it openly because it would undermine the source of living for ourselves as executives or managers. Otherwise you lose the race to grow in the career. Once you cross the management threshold, you are bound to live the lie, otherwise you lose it. And by the time you cross the management threshold, you are probably in debt of a home and have children who need an expensive school to make sure they have a network for the future ... bottom line, you have a bunch of ignorant managers who try to protect their ignorance by avoiding cross-collaboration and knowledge sharing between departments, while they have to say exactly the opposite to make sure they look good. And HR is in the same situation as the other departments.

While having a successful career, over a decade, Massimo realized that an open culture may be just a façade. Many companies don't practice what they preach, and this may actually be coming from the top possibly from the CXO level. The CEO may be the most miserable person in the company, acting as the figurehead, a 'yes man' for the shareholders. His direct reports did what was good for them rather than what was good for the team or organization. Often, 'business and cultural transformation' are just words used by consultants to market their services. However, on ground, the management practices mentioned in the company blogs and PR may not actually be exercised.

Massimo has had some of the best and most interesting jobs in the world. He has been an effective, hands-on skip manager and prefers to continue being the same because that is his way of making things happen, whether certain corporate factions like it or not. However, to say the least, he is neither blind nor stupid.

Massimo is aware that the overhead of a large company is mostly dedicated to keep up appearances. That is why one day came that he—partly motivated by a medical situation that required a life change—decided to take a step in a different direction: He invented an organizational transformation and laid off myself. He had actually deleted my position from the organizational structure, leaving a very ambitious new manager who suddenly saw her dream come true; to have her own department without going over the manager's head to grab an opportunity. The company was also very happy. They had an unexpected substantial saving for the next two years, that contributed to the bonuses of the top finance executives who had made the promise to the shareholders of achieving extra savings, at all costs (yes it sounds counterintuitive, and was not smart at all unless your purpose is just to get a bonus, but that is how it works in reality, no matter what is the official story).

Are you a skip manager too? Massimo's advice is to keep a constant meditative state. When it comes to work related matters, leave your heart at home, forget about personal agendas and navigate the corporate world impersonally, keeping in mind what the organization expects you to achieve. All efforts must strive to meet the key result areas within the boundaries of authority and ethics framework. That way new skips will have the time of their life and make money in the process. The less interested and detached you can be from the job itself, the longer you will keep it.

Last but not the least, a manager must enjoy his vacation, specially at a time when his/her own boss is away holidaying. However, it is important to remember to resume office a few days ahead of your boss in order to have a grip on the work that happened in your absence.

Two specific elements touched upon by Massimo are skipping levels and skipping jobs: Both need planning, patience and perseverance. Massimo was also faced by the ubiquitous question a few times during his career—what would happen if he went over his manager's head to see the boss's boss? In certain organizations, he discovered that such a step taken by an employee would be overlooked as long as the objectives set by the company were being achieved. In other organizations, however, he found that skipping levels to share your thoughts was as good as being asked to clear out your desk—especially if the reporting manager found out from his boss and not from you that you approached the skip manager without giving the reporting manager notice.

A manager who is vindictive, insecure and nervous about his team managers, he usually acts in two ways—He tries and get rid of the person who jumped levels or he colludes with the skip manager whom the team member approached and ensures that the skip manager doesn't act on any hearsay. In both these situations the team member either loses the job or is side-lined. Most skip managers, sadly, don't get coached on how to address the problems faced by employees that are a few levels below them. Corporate HR does not focus on the importance of the learning and developing for managers to effectively handle large teams. Most of the times, the higher-level managers are not even aware of the unacceptable behaviour of their subordinate managers when working with their reportees.

Taking a cue from Massimo's experiences, one must be aware of the organization's culture before thinking of setting up a meeting with the manager's boss to talk about the manager's inefficacy or even to generally seek guidance.

Before deciding to go over the manager's head for any reason whatsoever, one should ask themselves the following questions and consider the following nuggets of advice.

1. Does your skip manager know you well? Have you and your skip manager conversed before when your reporting manager was not around? If you have built a good rapport with your skip manager, chances are that difficult conversations will also be productive.

2. If you are dealing with an unqualified person as a manager who might also be undergoing some personal problems, try to find out whether the skip manager is already aware of these issues? In such cases, it's better to leave things alone to correct themselves rather than trying to jump over the manager's head.

3. In your organization, if the HR department seems to be regularly involved in the employees' welfare and is easy to approach, then it's always better to take your woes to the HR department instead of complaining to your boss's boss.

In one of my jobs, I had a manager who was an alcoholic; he spent hours in the evening at a fruit juice outlet under our office building while we waited for him for the evening review meeting. After an hour of waiting, he would stumble into the meeting having taken a few shots of alcohol mixed with the fruit juice. At times he seemed to be in full control of his faculties; however, at other times one of us had to drop him home. I had not been in the organization for long and was disturbed by the manager's behaviour. However, the manager's boss, our regional business head, didn't seem to notice anything wrong. This could have been because he actually didn't know about it or chose to ignore it because my reporting manager managed to get the desired results by overtaxing the team. In a span of six months, I had to drop the manager home on four or five occasions; as the manager's behaviour toward me started to become indulgent, I realized that he favoured such 'helpful' team members more than the others. It did occur to me to go over his head and report his unprofessional habit to his boss. However, my inner voice kept telling me that I was paid to be a sales executive and not a private investigator meddling with other people's personal habits and problems. Moreover, I decided that the regional head must rely on his own assessment and power of observation to evaluate the performance and conduct of a subordinate manager, rather than depending on my judgement. The biggest reason for listening to my inner voice was that I was not even sure if the regional manager would take my concern seriously. With this in mind, I focused solely on my work and didn't pay much heed to the manager's behaviour.

I applied what I learnt from the above experience when I was elevated to a managerial role. I learnt to have open conversations with my team letting them know that I was okay with them going to my manager. I just wanted them to be smart about what to take to the skip manager so as to avoid embarrassing themselves. Such openness in communication and a coaching-led approach worked wonders in developing a transparent relationship between me and my team.

Similarly, during my stint as a skip manager, I never tried to bypass the subordinate managers and give direct instructions to their reportees. Separately directing the managers' teams would have confused everyone and could have led my team members (including managers and their reportees) to question the managers' role if I was anyhow going to direct everyone by myself. That being said, some contact between the skip and the subordinate managers' reportees is always good so that the skip can get to know the reportees and vice versa. The contact can begin with exchanging cursory greetings and proceed to the reportees raising relevant and valid points during team meetings.

FURTHER READINGS

'Is It Ever OK to Go Over Your Boss' Head?' https://www.forbes.com/sites/dailymuse/2013/09/24/is-it-ever-ok-to-go-over-your-boss-head/#5c56ec1c4f0e

'Issue: CEO Conduct CEO Conduct - SAGE Business.' businessresearcher.sagepub.com › ceo-conduct

'Why Great Managers Are So Rare.' https://www.gallup.com/workplace/231593/why-great-managers-rare.aspx

# TRUTH ABOUT MANAGING LARGE TEAMS

Consider an organization that started with three people and a round table. The small team worked together; all three of them welcomed the two new people who joined their small circle. The two new people were also given workstations on the same table being used by the original three members of the organization. However, can you ever know how each person in your team likes to work? Here is an episode about the uncertainties that come up when a small venture grows to become a large organization.

Let's delve into this by taking the example of a new company whose co-founder is Ron; his role was to develop the technology for the venture. His passion was to develop solutions to complex problems using technology. His venture was doing well and in a year's time, the company took on more people as the workload grew and the customer base widened and spread to various regions. Ron took charge of the new and growing team. Along with the new members, he began developing a new product. Ron always believed in a strong balance between precision and speed and possessed a keen attention to detail. When the project was one-third complete, more people had to be hired since they needed a team with diverse competencies. Ron was quite blunt and straightforward with the whole team. However, Ron's way of working and his honest intentions didn't have the desired impact on the team. In every team meeting, Ron emphasized on the remaining work, but never recognized the progress made and the accomplishments of the people who had done well. Due to this, the team members started to put additional time perfecting their contributions rather than collaborating as a team.

After managing the team for two months, Ron realized he was not delegating enough and still micromanaging everyone's work. He had never bothered to understand the individual working styles and competencies of the team members. Hence, Ron didn't know how much to delegate and to whom and how much to tackle himself. The other co-founders constantly asked Ron about the project status since the new product launch was important for their business. As the team grew in number, the individual employees grew unclear about the key performance indicators, felt disconnected with the organization and many a times were micromanaged by the bosses. Ron acknowledged the issues; he clearly identified the priority projects, assigned the relevant people to different tasks, started a regular communication and review process and in turn ensured the teams felt a sense of belonging with the venture. While he was trying to sort of the management of teams as they grew, the other divisions like sales and marketing also grew in size as workload increased.

On the sales and marketing front at the venture, the business began to look up and four more people were hired. Eventually, the table fell short of space and more seating space, in the form of a few bean bags, had to be arranged. When even more people were added, the time came for the company to move to a proper office. During the beginning of the venture, the new employees were introduced personally to the existing team, processes and tools; they were told how the workplace functioned and where most things were kept. Two large pizzas were enough to feed the team. However, when new faces began to show every month, the introductions to the team and the office became more impersonal and mechanical.

Till the team size is around 20–25 people, management is not difficult. However, as this number increases, the management needs to understand that the current workplace routines may not work as effectively. The first indication of cramped space was when the founders asked everyone to assemble in the work room and realized that people were suffocating. That was the moment when the founders realized that their small company had outgrown the workspace as well as its current processes. They needed to work out new processes as the team's size and cultural dimensions began to expand.

With the founders trying to manage the team of 20 people, their time was squeezed dry. As the teams grew, unexpected issues arose including the increase in the quantum of communication required to get things done and the need to keep track of more decisions and the people associated with different projects and responsibilities. As the team size grew further, the work started to get clogged and decision-making slowed down. While the founders had maintained the core values of their management and leadership styles, the day-to-day routines began undergoing a significant change. They had to switch their management principal from direct to indirect management. Initially, when the team comprised four to five individuals, the founders could develop a personal rapport with each one of them. However, as the teams grew, the founders had to hire individuals with managerial experience to supervise individual contributors. The flipside here is that hiring wrong managers can have an adverse effect on the team immediately and eventually the company.

BASIC PRINCIPLES OF MANAGING LARGE TEAMS

There was a survey published by *Forbes* which stated that 65 per cent of employees would forego a pay raise if they could have their manager fired instead. Initially watching the teams grow exponentially can be overwhelming for the founders and they may begin to think that they are losing control. The best way to manage teams as they grow is to ensure that the right people are empowered to take charge and make decisions as and when required. As a team grows in number, managing effectively begins with trust.

No sooner than a manager feels that he has finally figured out the situation concerning management of his team, a new whirlwind engulfs him. In a growing organization, managers have to quickly adjust to handling team sizes that grow from 10 to 100 to 200 in no time. Leading a 10-people team is very different from leading a 50-people or a 100-people group. As the team grows, the need to unite them around a shared purpose as well as define behaviours, routines, culture and communication architectures becomes critical. Let us understand what these factors really entail.

- **Defining Behaviours.** Defining behaviours of employees involves outlining day-to-day transactions and interactions that set the rule of work. A manager should, at all times, know how effectively is trust and a collaborative spirit developing among his team members; how well is the team maturing, thriving and learning from each other's failures?
- **Defining Routines.** Defining routines is an important aspect of leading teams in order to be able to connect with the members to maintain enthusiasm and the urge to excel. Routines followed by companies to onboard and induct newcomers are important; employees can understand the company culture at an early stage through these inductions. Routines may also be set to include ways to enhance

connection between members across multi-locational offices by defining specific rituals to begin and end virtual meetings.
- **Defining Culture.** Culture translates to the ways adopted by management for developing a winning habit with a mix of strategic guidance and tactical insights on how to make the team win. It deals with defining the scope and practices to develop an environment that fosters innovation. This begins with setting the right tone and context for a respectful way of working and giving recognition to each individual in the team.
- **Defining Communication.** Defining communication is the core practice of developing and managing a high performing team. It helps prioritize and differentiate between tasks that an employee 'must do' and those they are 'good to do'. Communication needs a perfect balance of intensity and frequency—any imbalance creates confusion and lack of alignment to objectives. For some employees less frequent but highly intense communication works and for others more frequent but less intense bursts of communication helps keep them agile.

If you are an FTM, leading a smart and small team, it is advisable to start with defining your behavioural expectations from the team as well as defining a set routine for meetings, communications and team activities. It is also prudent to identify one or two team members who are a shade better than the rest in terms of a mix of strategic and operational strengths—Someone in the team should be shadowing and mirroring your virtues. Managing teams needs flexibility and adaptability at all levels—individual contributors, managers and skips. Small teams can be like an extended family where everyone knows each other well. The guiding principles to effective communication include the ability to create momentum, solving problems and faster turn-around time to decision-making.

Team Management Practices of the Tata Group

Dr Mukund Rajan describes some of the approaches adopted by the Tata Group when establishing teams across multiple locations and different cultural avenues, on the way to becoming a global organization.

It was an interesting learning experience for the Tata Group when their code of conduct document, first written in 1998 when the Group was mostly a domestic enterprise, was revised in 2015 when the Group had become a global enterprise. The globalization strategy included inorganic growth, including acquisitions like Jaguar Land Rover Automotive PLC (JLR) and Corus. With the acquisitions, almost 60–70 per cent of the Group's turnover came from outside India and the company witnessed a transition from being an Indian MNC to becoming a truly international company.

While developing the new globally applicable code of conduct, Dr Mukund realized that the understanding of clauses and interpretations could vary across cultures and countries where they were being implemented; for instance, whistleblowing was understood differently in different cultures. When the draft of the whistleblowing clause was first presented to managers in different countries, colleagues in France and Germany registered their issues with the clause. Their concerns were linked all the way back to the second world war and the perception of informers during that time. The actions of Nazi informers during the war were viewed as acts of betrayal and treason. The French and Germans associated some aspects of whistleblowing with those Nazi informers who were not trusted or respected in the society. This presented a huge contrast since whistleblowing, in most progressive corporate cultures, is meant to promote transparency and fearlessness in exposing malpractices prevalent in a company whereas some countries, due to prevailing prejudices in their culture viewed whistleblowing as an act of suspicion and looked down upon it. The Tata Group had to make it abundantly clear to all its employees in different nations that the whistleblowing clause was not intended to encourage employees to squeal on their colleagues but to call out anyone's actions that undermined the ethics and operations of the Group.

In any multi-locational and multicultural organization, the challenge is to ensure that there is a clear understanding of the company's practices, both operational and moral. If the path to ensuring meeting of the minds is not treaded carefully, the results can upset morale and lead to a lack of alignment with the management's thinking. A lot of time and effort needs to be invested in bringing people together mentally, if they are from different cultures. In such situations, critical matters need to be communicated directly from the top management. For organizations that have grown very fast or grown inorganically, embracing diverse cultures and nations, there may often be an initial lack of understanding among the new outposts about the parent organization's mission, vision and values. People are expected to self-accommodate and adjust to the ways of working post business acquisition and get over with the previous practices. However, if the ambition is to build a cohesive organization with complete alignment across geographies, then a lot of time should be spent with the people away from the headquarters. This ensures they feel that they are being embraced by the parent company. It also provides them assistance in understanding the purpose of the organization, its core focus and values and the career trajectory they can expect in the organization. Lack of such actions can lead to transactional behaviour that usually causes high attrition, since the employees don't feel a long-term commitment to the company. However, if they buy into the corporate purpose and it resonates with their personal values, then they become partners in the mission and not mere employees.

Educating the work force is very important. When JLR was acquired in 2007–2008, for several years many employees at the JLR shop floor in places like Birmingham were quite sceptical due to multiple changes in the ownership of the company. The Tata Group had to invest a lot of time and resources to align the leadership and the employees of acquired companies with Tata's way of working and communicate extensively on why they should feel proud to be a part of this large conglomerate. For any organization that has a large team spread across geographies and cultures, communication is critical, and the time and endorsement of top management is important and must be driven down to all the levels right from CXOs to individual contributors. If a sense of belongingness is not created, there can be a significant drop in the sense of ownership and responsibility, and eventually even in employee productivity.

Some employees may also have attitude problems, which may include a feeling of cultural superiority. At the official workplace, these might tend to be subdued since laws protect against discrimination. History does play a role and a lot of that is difficult to change (but not impossible) if someone insists on looking back to the past, including the era of colonial rule.

For FTMs handling multi-locational teams it's important to understand the background of the team members, including the operating managers and other individual contributors in the group; this shows that the new manager is interested in the existing team. A boss that spends time to understand the employees is respected and appreciated. A small greeting by the manager in the local language can be an effective ice breaker. If the manager wants his authority to be accepted by a large team, it is important for him to win their trust. Issues relating to time zones must be mitigated. Also, in the first year of becoming the manager, one must try to make periodic visits to different team locations and meet people personally.

MANAGING A TEAM: UP TO 25 MEMBERS

When there are only founders and co-founders, they work like a small nuclear family. The moment every founder has five or more people reporting to them, the structure begins to take shape of a joint family with more people and diverse preferences. There is one head of the family who is looked up to for strategic and tactical guidance. When the organization begins to grow beyond two levels, the attitude of employees and their cultural dimensions begin to play a significant role to the cohesion in the organization. Just like in an extended family, in a large team, tantrums are generally associated with employees who have been with the company since inception and may consider themselves above and beyond the new rules and practices being set up. In smaller teams, the discussions can be unstructured, ad hoc and with little emphasis on confidentiality. This happens due to the limited number of people involved and the winning/losing stakes are same for all. As the teams grow, the information needs to be filtered and for many it has to be shared on need-to-know basis. As the number of people on the team reaches the double digits, internal communication requires better structure and pattern. Check-ins with the reporting manager and the skip manager as well as team discussions and reviews require planning. Further, as the team grows, it becomes more diverse, both culturally and in relation to gender; everyone needs to adapt to and appreciate this diversity including the managers, both skip and reporting. As it's important to hire the right candidates during the initial stages of establishing the company, it's equally important to know how to manage them. Among the different hires, there will be some employees who will have become managers for the first time, and they will be learning how to manage teams for the first time. Hence the role of founders and core team members as skips becomes even more critical at this juncture. It is advisable to get help from expert coaches to mentor the FTMs in effective management. The founders will have to navigate through running the company, fundraising and other operational concerns and complications. As such, it is best for the leadership to not take on mentoring as well and seek specialist intervention.

MANAGING A TEAM: 50 TO 75 MEMBERS

As the team grows, managers and skips don't have the time to know everyone personally. So, the focus of the managers is directed toward creating and implementing ranks and flanks. The organizational architecture is the guiding light, which reforms the organization in a way to make the multitude of tasks happen in the scheduled time, even if it takes realigning people from one or various departments to ensure timely delivery of results. The managers need to define practices in order to be able to delegate more and scale up the output, along with constantly reinforcing the team's and organization's vision and values. Achieving this kind of cohesion becomes more complicated as the organization grows.

When the team size increases it is very important that the managers themselves also scale up. Managerial skills are challenged in unforeseen ways once the team size starts to take up more work and responsibilities. The role of subordinates as well as skip managers becomes more serious and impactful. An important aspect of ensuring that the team management is culturally aligned depends on how an existing manager, who might be exiting, onboards and handovers the tasks to an incoming manager who may or may not be coming from the same kind of business background and practice. Jeff Bezos, the founder of Amazon.com Inc. had given some words of wisdom on effectively handling teams: It's popularly known as the 'two-pizza team rule', which seems to suggests that the number of relevance of keeping direct reportees of a person should to be not be more than what two pizzas can feed; that is, approximately eight team members. The moment a manager has up to eight reportees, it's time to create a new team so that there is efficient and effective collaboration between employees. During the stage where a company is of growing in terms of manpower, specially from 25 to around 75 members, the management should make sure to have a good mix of internal promotions as well as external hires. All the managers need not be promoted from within the organization. Hiring a few managers from other universes lends a balance of growth and competitive spirit within the organization.

Geoffrey Lewis: Career Connector | TEDxSUU Speaker and Organizer | Public Speaker | Artist | Author

Geoffrey, a Stanford LEAD alumnus, leads Employer Relations for the Southern Utah University (SUU). He gives an account of his hiring at SUU, role of his Skip Manager in interviewing, onboarding and continual support till Geoff gets comfortable with the team, levels down and up.

Geoffrey related his interview experience with Dr Eric M. Kirby. When he interviewed Geoffrey, Eric was a skip manager. He asked Geoffrey the most surprising interview question and also provided him with one of the most exemplary onboarding experiences he has ever had.

After Geoffrey had successfully cleared the majority of the hiring process for the Career and Professional Development team at Southern Utah University, he had one last call scheduled with Dr Eric Kirby, the boss of his future boss and the Assistant Vice President for Student Affairs at the Southern Utah University. During the call, Geoffrey was asked a number of probing and relevant questions to ensure that he would be a benefit to the team, and then Eric surprised Geoffrey with the unexpected question: 'Why should we trust you?'

That was not a question Geoffrey had prepared for, so he started by thinking out loud and said: 'My initial, perhaps cynical, response would be that you shouldn't trust me, as you've never met me before.' Then, clearing his head, Geoffrey articulated, 'But if you ask anyone who has ever worked with me, they will tell you that I am professional and reliable, and that I care deeply about helping others succeed.'

When he later asked Dr Kirby about the purpose of this question, he replied that he intentionally asks this question to help determine how trustworthy a person is. If the individual gives an answer like 'My reputation speaks for itself,' without offering references, they likely have something to hide. If, however, they respond as Geoffrey did, referencing colleagues who will corroborate their record, then they are most likely trustworthy.

Personal Onboarding

When Geoffrey arrived to start work at Southern Utah University, his direct supervisor did a great job of getting Geoffrey up to speed. So, it came as a surprise when Geoffrey was informed that Dr Kirby had scheduled an hour-long meeting to sit down with him one-on-one to provide him with a strategic and long-term view of the work in the division. What surprised Geoff even more was that Dr Kirby spent the first half an hour just asking questions about Geoffrey to get to know him better including his hobbies and interests and questions about his family and the cities he had lived in before coming to Utah. Only after getting to know Geoffrey better did he introduce Geoffrey to the division's strategic focus. This gesture made Geoffrey feel that Dr Kirby truly cared about him as a person and not just as a business asset; it speaks volumes of how effective a skip manager can be, without potentially threatening the position of a subordinate or middle manager.

Geoffrey later learned that this practice of getting to personally know an employee was a division-wide policy. Each time the administration met with a student, whether in an official appointment or in line to buy lunch, they enjoyed asking getting-to-know-you questions to help the students feel valued and heard, and to help learn who they are so that the division could best support them. These questions include the following: Where are you from? What are your hobbies and interests? Why did you choose to come to our university? What are your dreams for the future?

Continued Support

Dr Kirby's involvement did not end with that first meeting. As a skip manager, he continued to instil a sense of involvement and belonging in Geoffrey, both through efforts directed at the whole team and helping him individually. Efforts directed at the whole team included graciously inviting them to his home for an ice-cream social and sending out weekly 'Thursday Thoughts' emails linking what he read that week to ways his reportees could improve the service provided to students. Individual help often took the form of helping Geoffrey address urgent situations when his direct supervisor was not immediately available, or when the weight of his Assistant Vice President title could leverage better results.

MANAGING A TEAM: 75 TO 100+ MEMBERS

When companies move from being a group of a few founders to 100+ employees, running the organization becomes more complex, demanding more authoritative and effective leadership.

As the team size grows from 75 members to 100+ members, the founders need to understand the importance of letting go. It's not humanly possible to oversee every strategy and each operation when the organization undergoes upscaling in business, locations and the number of employees. At this juncture, management skills of skip managers can make or break organizations. The founding members are now required to lead the managers and not be tempted to oversee the direct execution of strategy and operations by individual contributors—the way to stay ahead of the curve is effective skip management and empowerment of managers to lead the teams below them. With the addition of new managers, the founders and the core leadership team must not expect that every manager will be doing things exactly the way they did; as such, autonomy for managers, to a certain extent, becomes important. It can be a very rough situation and can lead to fragmentation in the team if the core leadership doesn't show confidence in the middle and subordinate managers and trust them to do the right thing and take right decisions.

One critical step, where the leadership can go wrong is hiring the right people at the right time and then retaining them. While hiring the first 20 employees, the core leadership of the company must look at the candidates with a hawk's eye, since the personnel initially hired at the company develops the company's culture going forward.

At this stage, the leadership must demonstrate complete trust in the managers by giving them autonomy and authority to make decisions, rather than personally directing both managers and their teams. This is the time to set management guidelines like clarifying how to lead teams and what the expected outcomes are as well as giving feedback and developing a culture of inclusivity. Chances are the teams may be based out of multiple locations by now; hence the important tools and guidelines for projects, budgets and systems and processes must be available to the managers anytime and anywhere (for instance, introduction of cloud framework can be applied at this stage). Making the managers feel empowered is critical at this stage. A mistake that the leadership should avoid is to not hire experienced HR and project heads. Both these functions need a balanced head when the team size reaches close to a hundred. Investing money to hire experienced professionals for project management and HR can save a ton of cost for the future. At this stage, the organization development can take a dangerous turn in case the founders and leadership team continues to be directive in approach rather than function in an advisory capacity. As founders and core leaders, one needs to understand the importance of empathy, communication and effective application of their hold over the company to be able to develop a truly world-class organization.

TRUTHS ABOUT HIRING TEAMS

While hiring the first 25 employees, the founders must try to be a part of every hiring so that the right expectations are set. Further, including advisors or investor representatives in the hiring process can ensure that the best candidates are onboarded. The involvement of the key personnel ensures that FTMs and HR know what the leaders are looking for in their employees. In this way, the HR and other managers can follow the example set by the leadership while assessing a candidate for a job.

When the company starts growing further, the founders and the core leaders need to start letting go and assess whether the managers are capable of carrying their mandate along with HR. In this transition period, the leadership may review *curricula vitae* (CV) and attend interviews of key hires and help the team in deciding the offer to be made. Here the role of a leader is to coach and mentor the managers throughout the decision-making process without imposing their opinions on them.

Once the company begins to reach the 100-mark, the role of the leadership intensifies as the need to keep the company intact arises. A team of 75 to 100+ employees indicates that the business is scaling up rapidly and so are the customer demands and expectations. The core management must let go of day-to-day decisions completely if the right guidelines for managers and employees have been put in place. If such guidelines are not set and the core management is unable to handover the reigns to the managers, the company will, more often than not, develop a non-progressive culture leading to a high rate of attrition at a time when talent is needed the most. At this juncture, the leaders have to play the critical role of a skip manager to keep the framework in place and plug the process gaps so that the junior managers don't act on assumptions.

THE FOUNDER'S ROLE WHEN THE COMPANY GROWS

As the size of the company swells and the company's establishments spread to different locations, the key personnel must pivot their management style from 'how to get it done' to 'what needs to get done'. When the manpower of the company is less than 100, the founders and key members of the company are right in thinking about every element of the business: the product, price, operations, bankroll, etc. However, as the company grows, the number of in-between managers should also grow with the company; the middle managers should be subject-matter experts who can be empowered to execute the higher management's vision by figuring out the how and deliver clear outcomes. The key personnel's job is now to make sure that the desired outcomes are abundantly clear. The expected outcomes don't just involve business results but also encompasses maintenance of the company's culture, reputation, ethics and the way businesses are transacted with internal and external stakeholders. The leaders who are not able to let go are responsible for creating a toxic culture of boilerplate micro-management, which leads to lack of trust and eventually brings organizational growth to a halt. It is important for founders to adapt to the changing roles for the sake of attracting and retaining the right middle management when the organization crosses the 75-employee mark.

MANAGEMENT ELEMENTS DURING THE COMPANY'S GROWTH SPURT

GENETIC CODING

Often, consistently high performing individual contributors become poor deliverers when they start managing teams. The new managers can develop something called the 'Special Snowflake Syndrome'. The key personnel feel that the managers hired during the initial stages of the company's development are snowflakes having a tendency of feeling special. They have a notion of being better than others and consider themselves to be ahead of the mainstream organizational expectations. These are the managers who would have worked as part of the core team with the company's founders, more privileged with lesser responsibilities. This can sometimes lead to excessive individualism and narcissism in these managers. As the company grows, the business and structural complexity also rises. The managers with Special Snowflake Syndrome can push back the change of levels, structures and resent the bureaucracy? As such, if these managers start displaying the tendency of 'not to be managed', the founders have a problem. The best situation is when existing managers, early in their careers, are coached to be mentors to incoming managers. This way both the existing and the incoming managers are able to respect the organization structures, rising up to the challenge of organization growth. A growing organization must pay attention to the behaviours of these employees and be open to letting go the people who are unable to align to the new ways of working.

I have coached a venture, which grew from a five-person team to an 80 people team in only a few years. The venture started out with just three people; Since they needed a coder, one of their earliest hires was a very hands-on engineer. However, in the initial six months, the founders realized that he was great in coding minimum viable products (MVP) and prototypes but lacked the patience to sort out bugs in the prototypes to launch a commercially viable version. Every time the engineer moved beyond creating an MVP, he struggled and had the tendency to give up since he was great with experimentation but lacked the structure to deliver finished products, which could be marketed. The founders tackled this problem by hiring three interns at a low cost and asked the coder to supervise and engage them to make the MVP marketable. Eventually, the coder was asked to lead the product development team. The team under this engineer was agile and worked well under his supervision; meanwhile, he was all too happy to keep experimenting with software coding, hence the arrangement worked out well. However, there could be a situation where the founders kept patience at the expense of losing time, money and opportunities, hoping that this engineer would eventually be able to deliver the project. In this alternative scenario, if the cost of waiting for the engineer to deliver could be avoided, the same could have helped the founders in hiring more people and get the task done.

REALIGNING MANAGERS

In the initial years of a company's life, FTMs are hired to lead a team of three to five people each. Once the organization starts to grow beyond 50 employees, the teams' sizes also start to increase, and the managerial capabilities of these FTMs is required to be revaluated. Some of these managers are bad at supervising large teams. At this stage, the teams should be realigned; some managers should be made to lead larger teams and some of them should be given important projects to handle as individual contributors. At this stage there must be a process put in place for managers to either qualify for upward mobility or become individual contribution specialists. However, the managers who are driven to become individual specialist contributors must not see this transition as a failure of management decision indicating any personal vendetta against the manager.

CROSS-FUNCTIONAL TENSIONS

Till the time a company has about 25 employees, the company functions on vertical deliverables more than cross-functional team effort and collaboration. As the company grows, new teams are established, new managers inducted, and the cross-functional working dynamics comes into play in full force. Here is where the managers and teams need to understand how to lead cross-functional teams and be able to work in one. Now is the time when product development, engineering, sales, marketing and support teams must fully align; it is difficult to achieve cohesion between multiple teams with different agendas, especially if the managers leading the different teams are unable to understand the dynamics required for working with other managers and their teams. The skip managers' intervention is required to ensure that independent teams are able to interact with each other keeping in mind the common purpose of the company. Any ego between peers has to be kept aside while partnering on different projects and tasks; the results are even better if the managements puts in place norms for effective partnership. Executive isolation starts when cross-functional teams develop irreconcilable differences, but the manager decides not to inform the executive management about it. The skip managers must swiftly resolve any conflicts between cross-functional teams so that there is no toxicity that can bring down a thriving company on its knees.

In an early-stage venture, many people multitask due to more work than the hands available can handle and also due to budgetary constraints. Employees in organizations more than 75 employees have four clear drivers: their work profile, people (managers and individual contributors), salary and location of work. When an organization grows to 100+ employees then the four motivators need to be balanced effectively. During the initial years of a venture, founders tend to burn cash reserves to hire people at higher salaries and offer them fancy titles. However, when the organization grows, the founders need to ensure that only those managers are retained who are able to work and inspire the growing teams. Many a times, managers and their teams may not be able to keep pace with the growing organization. When a venture grows in top speed, the teams need to keep pace. If they are unable to do so, it can lead to burnouts and poor outcomes at the workplace. Upscaling is as challenging as it is exciting.

ESTABLISHING TRUST

During the company's growth phase, the expert inputs of skip managers become critical. These inputs can achieve great results if applied correctly in letter and spirit. Skips can help in creating a sense of trust between subordinate managers and their reportees by adopting the practices discussed below.

A New Mindset

A skip manager must not consider every meeting with the subordinate managers and teams as only review meetings. This is the time to get to know the middle manager and his team better; be a problem solver with whom they can share the challenges they are facing, requiring the skip manager's experience and leadership.

Status and Success

If the middle manager insists that the meeting begins with a status update, then the skip must respect the decision. However, the skip manager may set the ground rules for the status updates to be precise and not last more than six to eight minutes. The meetings should also discuss recent success at work and how to imbibe them as best practices rather than only discussing problems at hand while indulging in blame games. Celebrating success is a great way to begin a meeting, with the skip manager, in a growing organization. Skips really appreciate hearing good news; it also sets an energetic and enthusiastic tone for the meeting and everyone becomes more comfortable lowering their defences.

Being Encouraging and Transparent

Skips must keep time for the middle manager and/or anyone from the team to present any new idea at hand. It can be something that can solve issues faster or an idea to diversify expand business. Encourage the middle manager to react to the ideas being tabled, in a transparent way, calling a spade as a spade.

Then the skip manager should react with their perspective on what would they like to support.

Upskill

Skip managers must emphasize the need for continuous training and upskilling. When organizations reach a growth spurt, the managers need to match the organization's pace. Effective skip managers often discuss a few leadership principles during meetings and encourage the middle managers and the teams to embrace such principles. A champion of change may be identified, a person who is empowered to institute the rollout to the larger group. This way, changes in ways of working are embraced voluntarily.

When Next

Meetings attended by skip managers can be periodic during the initial stages of the company's growth. The meetings can be scheduled to discuss specific agendas like effective communication, cross-functional team dynamics and addressing of rumours. It is quite possible that most meetings need a follow-up discussion, hence, the date and time for such meetings must be set in advance for the sake of continuity.

The Three Personas of a Successful Organization

Balaji Ramakrishnan is a Stanford LEAD Alumnus with 20+ years of experience in the IT Industry, working in multiple geographies and cross-cultural teams. He has successfully led large teams for critical business transformative initiatives and has consistently delivered positive results. He is currently employed in a leadership role in Adobe IT, India and is responsible for business system integration of Adobe acquired companies. He talks about three personas of a person's professional life in a company and how these personas can be leveraged as opportunities to build great organizations. The three personas are (a) skip manager, (b) middle manager and (c) individual contributor.

It is imperative to understand why a leader initiates a skip-level meeting. There may be three reasons for this:

(a) Skip-level meetings are arranged as a formality by some to demonstrate that the leader is accessible.

(b) Skip-level meetings are initiated out of curiosity to identify hidden talents for future growth of the company.

(c) Skip-level meetings may be scheduled by the leaders who want to know the ground-level reality if they are not comfortable with the results being achieved by the middle managers or if they are not happy with the way the middle managers are overseeing their projects.

Keeping in mind these three key reasons, let us see how different personas handle the skip-level meetings.

Skip Manager: Natural Gainer

The persona who gains most from these meetings is the skip manager.

If the reason for scheduling the meeting is the first reason stated above, the skip manager can use these occasions to get a pulse of what is happening on the ground directly from the individual contributors on the ground and can reconcile their claims against what he has been hearing from the middle managers directly reporting to him. These meetings help the skip manager identify lead indictors on the good outcomes, the ones that need to be maintained or ignored and the potential issues that may need attention.

If the reason for scheduling the meeting is the second reason stated above, the skip meetings are a wonderful opportunity to evaluate the potential of individual contributors. This way the skip manager can himself identify and reassess the top talents who have been recommended by the middle managers as the future leaders in the company.

If the reason for scheduling the meeting is the third reason stated above, the skip managers should provide a safety net to individuals, who are giving them valuable insights about the challenges that are being faced on the ground level because of the reporting manager. The skip manager should be tactful in their dealings with the reporting managers and not reveal the identity of the individual contributors to their reporting managers; instead the skip managers should use these insights to ask the middle managers more probing questions and zero in on the issues that need his/her attention. This will provide more confidence to the individuals to bring in genuine issues, that are not being addressed on the ground, to the skip manager's notice. This may also be helpful for the skip manager to identify the individuals who can be groomed as potential leaders for the company.

Middle Manager

Whenever a skip-level discussion happens, the persona that naturally feels insecure is the middle manager. To be able to handle the situation better, the middle manager must understand the reasons for holding these discussions.

One opportunity that the meeting presents is to identify and prep the key talents in the team for these engagements, so that the identified individuals get to showcase their talents and impress their skip manager. This is a win-win-win situation. The skip manager gets to assess the talented people in the organization; the middle manager ends up helping their boss identify the talented people in the organization;

further, since the middle manager identifies the talent, he/she creates a more loyal network for themselves in the organization since they have been key players in helping the individuals succeed in the organization; moreover the middle manager's boss will see him/her as a confident manager, who does not feel insecure. Lastly, the individuals benefit from the growth opportunity.

Balaji shared a simple but powerful approach practiced by one of his managers, who used to seat top talents in the organization just opposite his cabin, so that he had a clear view of these individuals. He did this on a rotational basis under which all the key talents got the opportunity to work under his direction observation as well as get the opportunity for small talks in the hallway with him. This helped him create opportunities for showcasing the individual talents in his team to his boss.

If the reason for organizing skip-level meetings is reason number three, then one needs to be on their toes and get their act together, since chances are that the skip manager is looking to determine the issues being faced by a particular team and why; what are the various challenges being faced by the team on ground; and how various issues are being mismanaged. However, this is not a reason to feel disheartened—there is always an opportunity to right wrongs!

The middle manager can encourage the team to voice the issues faced by the team members along with the steps being taken by the manager to overcome those issues or the course of action to settle the issues in the team. This will help the middle manager achieve two objectives, which are mentioned below.

(a) The middle manager will avoid coming across as a vulnerable person to his/her team, since he/she has displayed that they are not afraid to voice team issues in front of the skip manager.

(b) You are able to garner support from your team to voice the issues so that the leader understands its serious implications.

As the middle manager tries to achieve these two objectives, it may also lead to a self-introspection about how he/she needs to handle things in a better way by understanding the root cause of the challenges on ground. The middle manager will be able to demonstrate to the team that he/she is serious about taking corrective actions, getting management attention to listen to the issue and offer support.

Individuals

The third persona in these meetings is the individual contributor; they are the ones scheduled to have a discussion with the skip managers. Often, the individual contributors don't understand the leadership style or the intention of the skip manager for scheduling these meetings—the lack of understanding can be attributed to limited access/exposure to the skip manager on a day-to-day basis—thus, many times they end up airing their grievances—including not getting promotions, not getting to work on good assignments or bias in the team—very emphatically and emotionally. These issues generally tend to be dismissed by the skip manager and directed back to the reporting manager to resolve.

Due to the uncertainty of agenda and his or her own frustrations, the individual contributor misses an opportunity to make a positive impact on the skip manager, and in the process ends up aggravating his reporting manager as well. To avoid this from happening, the individual contributor should, instead, use the meeting as an opportunity for advancement by following the guidelines discussed below.

(a) Talk about the good work the team is doing despite operating under multiple constraints.

(b) Explain your perspective on how the challenges can be addressed and politely ask for advice, budgets and resources.

(c) Focus on sharing meaningful insights with the skip manager, that will help the team to be motivated for delivering higher performance levels.

(d) Don't backbite about your reporting manager. However, if you are prompted, be watchful of sharing your opinion about your manager with hard facts/examples. This is the most difficult part about meetings with skip managers, as individual contributors generally find it difficult to handle/understand the dynamics between the reporting manager and the skip manager.

Once the skip manager starts seeing value in the time spent with you, more meetings will follow over time, which, if approached with tact, will help the skip manager gain more confidence in you and he will eventually help you grow in the organization.

In this whole process, it is also important to understand how to handle your manager. Try to ascertain whether the reporting manager is feeling insecure. If he is feeling insecure, be open about the conversation you had with the skip manager and relay the good things that were mentioned by you to the skip manager in the meeting about the team, the challenges faced by the team, the reporting manager's help in resolving the challenges and the additional help needed from the skip manager. This will ensure that the reporting manager feels more confident and will view you as his supporter/partner.

However, if the meeting is more focused on the skip manager prompting you to share more about your reporting manager, it is not necessary for you to discuss the contents of the meeting with your manager because you don't know how it will be received by the reporting manager and you may end up losing support from your manager as well as the skip manager.

The overarching truth is that when organizations grow, they transform at a fast pace. During this period, the employees should not get caught in a turmoil and lose sense of trust in the company. The leadership, skip managers and middle managers must ensure that the teams are still able to see consistency in their day-to-day actions. Ability to promote stability in the wake of growth is the biggest test of leadership. The skip managers should not act in a way that makes the teams feel discouraged and undervalued at any point in time. The personal and professional connections established through skip meetings at regular intervals will help the middle managers and individuals at every level stay informed and invested in the company during big transitions.

With growing teams, managers need to evolve as strategists and generalists than being merely subject-matter experts. The important factor is how to get the best out of diverse groups of people. Take for example, my interim MD assignment in Sony Ericsson was to build and lead a USD 200 million organization. As all other CEOs, I was also not an expert across all crafts of sales, design, technology, corporate communications, finance and culture. My strength was in commercialization of technologies and handling people. I used to deal with the leadership and their teams across Japan, Singapore, Sweden and UK, entrusted with keeping the sails of the soaring. My assignment entailed dealing with people located in multiple time zones, people from variety of cultural backgrounds and ethnicities, various workflows with inherent opportunities and challenges. Getting them all to work together toward a common objective was imminent, which happened by reminding them about a sense of purpose. While the organization grows and earns respect, ultimately, it's the people and their equation with each other in the company that makes or breaks organizations.

FURTHER READINGS

Lussier, Robert. 2018. *Management Fudamentals: Concepts, Applications, & Skill Development*, Chapter 8. Thousand Oaks: SAGE Publications.

'Why Do Managers Forget They Are Human Beings?' https://hbr.org/2018/01/why-do-so-many-managers-forget-theyre-human-beings

Saporito, Thomas J. 2012. 'It's Time to Acknowledge CEO Loneliness.' https://hbr.org/2012/02/its-time-to-acknowledge-ceo-lo

BREAKING THROUGH EXECUTIVE ISOLATION

It's lonely at the top—a phrase many senior management professionals embrace and usually mention in friendly chats. Being lonely is not by will but happens by design when executive isolation is in play.

During one of my middle-management level corporate assignments, a colleague of mine, Joy, joined me for coffee. He clearly appeared frustrated, uncertain and confused. Joy narrated:

I had to present facts of a project to my manager's manager and his peers in a meeting yesterday. It took me three sleepless days and nights to bring all the material together. I got the guidelines from my manager and was completely sticking to them. However, few hours before the scheduled presentation, my manager asked for a final review of the presentation. I didn't understand the need for it since everything had been reviewed a lot of times already; I needed time to pull myself together since I was to present to the skip-level manager and his peers. However, to my surprise, during the final review, my manager started to change the tone and impact of certain outcomes being presented. The manager started introducing unnecessary white lies in the presentation. The most surprising part was when he asked me to downplay the suggestions presented in the last two slides to improve efficiency and instead wanted me to end the presentation with the problems being faced.

In Joy's opinion, the last few slides discussing the ideas for improvement were the crux of the matter and they had to get management buy in for implementing them. Instead the manager told him that since they had the solutions figured out, they don't need to relay them to the higher management so soon. He went in to assure Joy that the amendments suggested by him will be well received by the attendees. He also told Joy that the skip manager and his peers would prefer Joy to focus on areas on which action can be taken immediately. Hence, he wanted Joy to showcase the solutions to smaller and tactical issues, and not the solutions that they had already developed for bigger challenges at hand.

Joy was very puzzled with this advice. The skip manager had personally asked for this meeting and had invited the higher management to the meeting. He had seemed very interested to know the whole nine yards and not just the operational stuff. But now he was asking Joy to downplay the important part of the presentation and that too at the last minute. Joy was perplexed and wondered what was going on. Some of the solutions they originally wanted to propose could have potentially become best practices for the organization at large. How could Joy's manager not understand something so fundamental?

I listened to him, but at that time offered no advice, since in my career as well such episodes had happened. Individual contributors and FTMs often face awkward moments when their immediate managers want to orchestrate the communication to be presented to their own boss. Senior executives often get shielded from the organizational challenges and associated data by their reportees; sometimes it is by design and may happen due to the acts of the senior management itself. Those who feel lonely at the top may be undergoing executive isolation where they feel left out; the middle managers are a part of the cause of executive isolation. Skip managers are eager to cultivate connections with the managers reporting to them to remain a part of the show, feel involved and not disconnected.

Contrary to this, middle managers prefer their bosses to not be over exposed to the levels below, causing executive isolation.

EXECUTIVE ISOLATION: A REAL ISSUE

The phenomenon of executive isolation is not new: It is a common practice of most managers to keep their bosses isolated from the levels below them. This is loosely known in the management circles as 'Executive Gatekeeping or Executive Isolation'—a state of feeling separated from the action and people within the organization. The Harvard Business Review published a study on CEOs in which they revealed that half of the CEO's who were interviewed as part of the study felt isolated and 61 per cent of those CEO's mentioned that the isolation makes them feel lonely and directly affects their critical and strategic thinking abilities.

Five years after he took charge as the CEO of Apple, an interview with Tim Cook was published in 2016 by the Washington Post. In that publication, Tim Cook talked candidly about the issues and challenges of running Apple, one of the world's biggest organizations. 'It's sort of a lonely job, he said. While he didn't mean it literally, Tim Cook indicated that isolation, which develops into loneliness, is the hard truth of CXOs jobs.

Most organizations, as they start to grow in size and locations, have employees, right from executive assistants (EA) to reportees, who start shielding the higher-ups at the company from a lot of communication and information they feel is of no use to the higher management. Initially the intent is to make the best use of the management's time and filter low-value activities so that the senior executives can focus on what actually requires their attention. However, eventually, the filtering leads to the higher management being kept from valuable developments as well; managers also begin doctoring the communication from their teams to the skip managers. Such practices of executive isolation infect the company's culture as leaders are shielded from issues faced by company personnel. They are not able to receive new ideas related to dynamics at work which could have contributed to more effective and timely decision-making. Instead, the senior executives receive filtered and censored information, which reportees feel they would like to hear rather than what they should actually hear. A lot of managers do numerous pre-meetings with their staff before the reviews or discussions happen with higher order executives. This is also dependent on the intent and urge of senior leaders to be connected to the right information.

Overall, the organization looks up to a CEO to be the driving force behind achievement of the company's set goals. It's the CEO's responsibility to make decisions, facilitating and shaping an entire business. Many a time, the CEO and his/her direct reportees are not made aware of the real organizational problems and the associated data. Eventually the decision-making personnel starts to receive limited and filtered information about the health of operations and the status of employees and customers at large. Eventually executive isolation leads to a dissatisfied top brass, which eventually becomes vulnerable and susceptible to attrition.

A strong, unabated executive isolation can indeed compromise effectiveness of leadership, leading to compromise in decision-making.

As a senior executive, breaking through executive isolation is necessary but not easy. For starters, one needs to first accept that executive isolation is and will always remain in play. Thereafter, one should spend some time to find ways of breaking it and implement the strategy for breaking it and then issue ground rules to their reportees so that the isolation does not get out of hand again and the senior executives can remain connected to the real work. This can happen by maintaining a culture of regular skip-level meetings, the occurrence of which is known to managers at all levels. Meeting with managers from other parts of the organization brings true cross-functional work dynamics in play and the executives can get unvarnished reports and views during spontaneous dialogues.

Within organizations, individual contributors and FTMs often don't approach skip managers and senior executives. This is because of the general understanding as well as the rumours heard from the executive's staff about the do's and don'ts to be practised with the senior leadership. One must not take all such rumours on face value. Sometimes rumours heard through the grapevine become reasons leading to executive isolation since the practices to be followed with senior leadership are usually not officially informed to the staff members. One should use their own judgement on how to communicate with skip managers, which begins with having the courage to put forward your opinion on the issues being discussed in meetings with your manager and his bosses. If you have some intelligent thoughts to be shared during a conversation, then don't hold yourself back. Be concise, precise and meaningful when trying to contribute in management meetings. If you get acknowledged as someone whose ideas are worth considering, it's a win for your manager as well for having developed good talent in the team. While taking your manager in confidence, always give them unadulterated information regarding any new ideas or challenges and the solutions without any manipulation. A sensible thought is always well received by one ear or another.

The first requirement of reducing the practices and impact of executive isolation is to encourage a culture of developing talent in the organization that appreciates the importance of skip-level engagements and does not delve into the practice of executive isolation.

Skip-level Management Practices: The Case of Anirvan Sen

Anirvan Sen, based out of Netherlands, is the founder of Fifth Chrome. He has over 25 years of experience and specializes in 'lean' management, 'agile', mergers and acquisitions through business scale-up and transformations. Anirvan has worked extensively in Asia, Europe, Middle East, Africa, UK and the US with marquee companies like GE, Coca Cola, AkzoNobel, Stryker and Gilead Sciences.

With a broad experience in leading and instituting organizations, Anirvan is passionate about developing talent through skip-level management, eventually reducing executive isolation.

It was a typical grey Dutch day. Nothing exciting for most people. But Anirvan was excited because his boss's boss was traveling from their global headquarters to Netherlands that day and he was scheduled to meet her for the first time since he started his new role. Being high-potential employee, Anirvan was promoted into a fast-track role to leadership opportunities. The meeting was part of something called a skip-level management meeting.

This meeting was unusual in many ways compared to meetings in his prior jobs. His prior meetings tended to be ad hoc and were primarily introductive or information gathering meetings. Moreover, instead of being one-on-one meetings, they were usually team meetings. because of his insecurities.

Since Anirvan himself had grown in his career from a managerial to a CXO role, he could see that all the middle managers were not keeping him informed about a lot of details. Some of them even ensured they spoke to Anirvan on a need-to-know basis, mostly only for certain approvals. He claims that he didn't realize the importance or requirement and construct of the meetings back then. But over the years, he understood the real power of skip-level meetings and how to reduce executive isolation. Skip Management seems to be one of the most critically acclaimed modern-day management methods to develop talent.

What Is Skip-level Management According to Anirvan

There are various definitions that exist for skip-level management. Most of them roughly translate to the management practice adopted by the senior management where they bypass the intermediate/middle management and interact directly with people who are either part of the junior management of the company or are in non-managerial positions.

This broad definition includes all sorts of interactions between the two groups including ad hoc meetings, team meetings and side meetings at team events. However, Anirvan includes the culture of talent development as a part of his experience of skip-level management. In his opinion, this component also amplifies the real essence of skip-level management and how to mitigate executive isolation issues.

The description that Anirvan subscribes to most is the one that describes skip-level management as a special management technique; one that is used by senior and executive management to interact with high-potential employees and key personnel from junior management and non-managerial positions. This interaction provides huge visibility to junior employees and provides them with opportunities to be mentored by the senior management and create a personal connection with them. For the senior management, this framework provides a window to high-potential and upcoming talent in the company that needs to be groomed and mentored.

Anirvan classified to have skip meetings only when it was needed as a part of the structured grooming process of the teams. He has seen different forms of skip-level meetings. Most of them are get-to-know each other meetings. However, some are part of a structured mentoring process; this is where he sees the maximum value skip-level management can impart—to coach, train and mentor bright employees without being isolated from them by middle managers.

At this juncture, I would like to introduce a word of caution for the readers who are currently stakeholders in the organizational set-up discussed above as well as readers who are working towards the same. Skip-level management is a great tool for talent management, but it's not necessarily the most effective tool for performance management. Talent grooming is a multi-year program that requires a minimum commitment of 18–24 months, whereas performance management can usually be managed at an annual level and in some cases, even twice a year. There is a strong overlap between the two and the management should exercise caution and understand this crucial difference between the two at the time of execution.

Benefits of Reducing Isolation through Effective Skip-level Management

Many organizations around the globe have successfully utilized this technique to increase their bench-strength comprising of the next set of leaders for the organization. When implemented formally in a defined structure, skip-level management can provide several benefits to an organization.

- **Visibility.** It provides tremendous visibility for aspiring junior resources and can serve as a remarkable motivational boost for these individuals. The interactions with the senior management also help these individuals to polish their presentation skills, acquire executive presence and sharpen their communication competencies.

- **Structured grooming.** Skip-level management is helpful in structured and effective grooming through step by step plan for multiple interactions. The individuals identified as the up-and-coming talent actively start being considered for new roles and stretch assignments by the senior management.
- **Leadership pipeline and executive thinking.** This benefit is an obvious one. A structured approach to talent grooming creates a solid pipeline of future leaders for the organization. Through skip-level interactions, individuals get to understand the vision and objectives of senior management. They get to socialize with them and are introduced to the means and ways of senior management's thinking, plans and their way of execution of these plans. Additionally, these individuals may get opportunities to contribute their inputs and, in some cases, even participate in the execution. This way they can deeply entrench themselves in senior-management initiatives.

Execution Challenges

For all the advantages of skip-level management, poor execution remains a big challenge. Irrespective of the size, industry, geography and maturity of a company, implementing effective skip-level management is an initiative that needs comprehensive strategic thinking and a detailed rollout plan. Anirvan claims to have witnessed several initiatives started with great fanfare only to die away within the first year of their inception, mainly because of interference from the middle managers. However, hindrance posed by middle managers is not the only reason for the failure of skip-level management initiatives. There are several factors that create these challenges, some of which are discussed below.

- **Alignment.** One issue arises when the program implementation is not fully aligned with talent development strategies. Without a proper delineation of expectations and outcomes, these meetings often become endless talkathons on good-for-nothing topics. After the initial introduction calls, the next set of meetings should be structured as mentoring sessions and talent grooming sessions with definite outcomes in mind. These outcomes should be meticulously captured and managed as per the talent development guidelines.

- **Authority of intermediary management.** Undermining the authority of intermediary management is another challenge associated with these skip-level management programs. Mid-level managers are generally assigned specific responsibilities and their scope of management in respect of the teams is set. However, improperly implemented skip-level frameworks can lead to discussions and actions that can seriously undermine the responsibilities of the mid-level managers.

  Once a certain level of comfort is developed with skip-level managers, junior resources feel emboldened and they start voicing their opinion about their manager's work and authority. Senior management, in their curiousness, often forget the ethos of the structure and actively encourage sharing of more information. This can have a damaging impact for the organization. Skip-level managers must remain vigilant about the untoward attempts of junior employees to foray into discussions on their reporting managers.

  There is, however, a special instance where information about the performance of mid-level managers is sought through a skip-level discussion with the reportees. This usually happens when the mid-level managers underperform their own tasks and are unable to deliver requisite results.

- **Suspicious mid-management.** Mid-level managers are not always kept in the loop of the interactions that take place between their managers and their direct reportees; many mid-level managers struggle to adapt to this culture. They don't feel comfortable with the situation and often begin to get suspicious of the whole program fearing their authority being compromised.

  Before embarking on a skip-level management program, organizations must take mid-level managers in confidence, walk them through all the details of the program and most importantly, ensure a certain level of transparency to keep their trust.

- **Politics and manipulation.** The most lethal challenge of all is that of corporate politics and manipulation. Many senior managers are adept in such practices, and they end up abusing skip-level management to further their own cause and beliefs. Not very easy to detect, politicking can easily destroy the essence of this management method.

- **Sign off note.** Skip-level management needs a considerable amount of effort, commitment and discipline from its participants. An organization must create a robust framework for the same, assign specific roles and responsibilities, coach senior management on how to lead their programs, put policies and guidelines in place and most importantly, have a neutral and yet effective program governance in place.

Additionally, if an organization already has a well-established talent management function within their HR and leadership teams, it is likely to be easier for them to implement skip-level management programs.

In general, this program can be best utilized by large companies and some mid-sized companies. Most small companies and mid-sized companies tend to struggle to enforce the required discipline needed for the program; even if they are able to successfully implement the program, they find it difficult to maintain the structure of the program.

Even large companies that do not have an open and transparent work environment, struggle to derive the benefits of this program. Without trust between different management layers, this program becomes a non-starter.

Sign Off Note

Effective skip management, that can break executive isolation barriers, can benefit from an employee empowerment program, which can create a lot of value for organizations. It can help build a robust leadership pipeline; it can harness the aspirational energy of junior resources; management can get fresh perspectives on organizational objectives and create a congenial environment for interaction between different layers of the organization.

On the other side, such initiatives and programs have significant overheads and require disciplined approach. Without tangible benefits being visible quickly, organizations may struggle to get the right buy in from different stakeholders and find it challenging to keep up the discipline over a prolonged period of time.

Every organization is different. Before embarking on this program, organizations must question themselves to see if a skip-level management approach is the right one for them or not. They must thoroughly assess the needs, the benefits and the commitment required to implement this program, apart from fostering an environment of comfort and trust.

Skip-level management is a powerful talent management tool. Implemented the right way, it can significantly galvanize talent development programs and provide an envious competitive edge.

THE NEED TO ADDRESS EXECUTIVE ISOLATION

Middle managers, dealing with imposter syndrome, are generally insecure. Many middle managers suffer from imposter syndrome. This syndrome is a cause of managers not able to internalize their accomplishments and believe they are not worthy of being credited with achievements. Impostor syndrome was initially called a 'impostor phenomenon' in the 1970s by Suzanne Imes, PhD and Pauline Rose Clance, PhD. The two psychologists were studying the confidence levels in working women. Their research brought out the fact that many high-achieving women lacked self-acknowledgment of their success and had a pessimistic frame of mind. Over a period of time, it has been realized that imposter syndrome impacts managers irrespective of their gender. This leads to a feeling of inadequacy, self-doubt while thinking that their achievements are happening by fluke. Such managers are good at their work, but do not always get far in their careers because of this insecurity. In many cases, the insecurity leads them to isolate the higher management from the teams below. There are managers that have relevant college degrees and a well-paying job; a lot of them were even promoted out of turn initially, being high performers. Yet, these managers lament about not being good enough, not for seeking adulations but because they feel insecure about their reportees as well as their managers. A voice in their head keeps telling them that they are not good enough or smart enough and are unqualified for the position and achievements that have come their way. In an attempt to overcome this syndrome, such managers become perfectionists and workaholics, but also end up creating a divide between the skip managers and the junior employees. The managers that deal with imposter syndrome start practising executive isolation as a way to combat the feeling of not being good enough. In such cases, skip managers should engage in a lot of positive talk with subordinate managers to help them overcome their struggle with imposter syndrome. For leaders, executive isolation can wreak havoc in their lives and careers if not addressed effectively and in time. It can compromise decision-making and overall effectiveness of a leader. Here is how senior management can address executive isolation.

RECOGNIZE AND ACKNOWLEDGE

Executive isolation is not a seldom occurring phenomenon; there are many managers who go through this commotion—some are able to overlook it but for others it begins to impact their performance at work. However, many senior leaders believe acknowledging they are feeling isolated is a sign of weakness or a lack of competency to perform their functions effectively. However, recognizing that there is a feeling of isolation is a beginning itself. Just recognizing the feeling can help figure out the cause of such feelings and help to mitigate the issues and behaviours leading to executive isolation.

BIRD'S EYE VIEW OF ACTION ON GROUND

Professionals talk about various strategic views in business from a firm's perspective. The 'helicopter view' and the 'bird's eye view' are two commonly known phrases, and then there is the actual action and operations referred to as the 'battlefield'. As one grows in the organization chain, the battlefield starts to be distant as the higher-level strategic view starts to gain importance. The battlefield is where all the work and action happen, where the middle managers as front-line leaders make the business and operations run in line with company targets. Helicopter or bird's eye view is visible to the senior executives who have high positions in the company and are able to see the bigger picture and help the frontline leaders with resources and guidance. The most mindful and emotionally successful leaders adapt to swing the right balance between their bird's perch on the top and the battlefield at the ground. Avoiding executive isolation can be like being on a reality show, sometimes if you see a meeting going on, just open the door and stand in the alley in a friendly manner merely to listen to the meeting discussions or ask the Chief Sales Officer (CSO) to take you on a few sales calls. Essentially the subordinate managers should know that you can jump into their territory in a non-threatening way at any time. To remain involved, being connected to the inner working of the organization's business is important. The intent is not to alarm the people with your presence or intimidate them. Leaving the confines of your cabin to connect with others works as a fantastic strategy to overcome executive isolation and helps in developing engagements across verticals in the organization.

CREATE CHALLENGES AND CONSTRUCTIVE DISAGREEMENTS

Rather than just asking the managers to give you regular reports in a pre-defined format, create higher order achievement challenges for them. Eventually this constructive approach trickles down from the managers to the teams.

If the voices in your managerial ranks and teams are silent, it means they either lack psychological safety or feel that challenging the higher management has negative repercussions and induces judgement.

If, as a senior management staff, one is not experiencing push backs, then it is safe to say that his/her team has landed into the 'Yes Man' zone. The subordinate managers with the Yes Man syndrome only relate 'good news' to managers and just report about things going right in the battlefield, viz., the actual operations of work. Such managers always tend to keep the senior executives at the bird's eye level. The Yes Man managers also don't feel comfortable confronting the senior managers and they don't speak up even when a crisis is looming upon them, hence, delaying decision-making. Eventually, along with causing executive isolation, these managers also start prioritizing their career over personal and professional integrity.

PEER-TO-PEER LEARNING

Often, the professionally isolated executives are unable to move outside their limited perspectives, which stifles their growth professionally and personally. In order to bring a variety of continuous learning avenues, senior executives must get an external perspective. Such a practice is very critical to overcome isolation. By reaching out and joining a peer learning group, the senior executives break away from an environment that can be manipulated and controlled by subordinate middle managers. The peer learning group can be a network of industry agnostic executives dealing with similar challenges with an eye on the future. Discussions amongst various industry peers as an intersection of ideas and concepts leads to cognitive diversity that can bring about practices for innovation. Executive isolation manifests when viewed with a limited perspective; it can be countered by developing a peer learning ecosystem for getting a fresh perspective and scope.

While senior leaders have a busy schedule with multiple meetings every day, one must make it a habit to visit the floor where the ground level battle is fought. During the week, meetings for brainstorming and creative constructive conflict should be set up, in a manner which is not threatening to the subordinate managers. Such measures tend to reduce executive isolation and setup the leadership for new paradigms of success.

Executive isolation is the new normal and a lot of skip-level management principles are in play.

SILOS MINDSET

The Silo structures are defined as a work practice where departments or functions want to stick to their job descriptions and do not wish to share information with other divisions and departments to harbour collaboration, within the organization. This silo-based mentality in the current times of need for agility, drastically reduces efficiency in operations and at many levels impacts employees and managers' morale. Eventually it can lead to the company culture becoming more like one person passing the baton or his responsibility to the other under the pretext of particular task not being a part of his role and responsibility. Silo- and structure-led isolation can happen at any level; the worst case is when it leads to distrust, lack of cooperation and the shutting of doors to share relevant information. Eventually it fractures the fabric and culture of an organization, impeding progress at large. Breaking down the silo mindset needs two things—a common mission and a sizeable one. The transformative world of today's businesses can learn from the defence forces' handling of the unfortunate 26/11 terrorist attack of Mumbai—with a common mission and sizeable one, all the sections of Indian military forces realized that when the when the enemy at the gates is quite evolved, mature and progressive, decentralized old age tactics of working have to be set aside. India had the best task forces, intelligence ecosystem and paramilitary at its disposal; they put their hierarchy and differences aside to successfully ensure the safety of civilians. Eventually, the 26/11 attack became a global collaborative effort of with multiple nations offering their intelligence to quash the terrorists. It's an example of a mission that was clearly understood by all and didn't mean different things to different stakeholders.

Drawing the analogy to the business world, structures are formed in an organization to facilitate division of communication and work. A business-unit approach is a decentralized and delegation-led system that has divisions of experts in particular zones. However, the same system that assures smooth functioning of businesses can also lead to siloed structures and executive isolation when the organization starts to grow in size and expands geographically.

A silo mindset often arises at several organization levels and eventually becomes an integral part of the organization's functioning, making it more inward looking about how the department is functioning, more than how the functioning impacts the stakeholders, becoming a major obstacle that challenges growth.

Even though the senior leadership is friendly and conducive to divisional co-operation, the managers helping the platoons on the front-line can hold forth in silos. Managers with such mindsets hesitate to cooperate and share information with other divisions and teams. They limit themselves to a micro framework of deliverables and pass on this culture to their teams as well. Such siloed divisions only work towards fulfilling their immediate responsibilities, while assuring the senior leadership that the long-term goals are very much in sight. With such lack of harnessing cross-departmental synergies, eventually the organization's success is hampered, and they fail to seize growth and expansion opportunities.

Silos tilt the balance of power only to a few players, which in turn makes executive isolation more prominent. The power centres in the ranks can add to increasing mistrust and lack of collaboration between the units that must perform together in the larger interest of the organization. In the absence of collective goals and senior leadership's knowledge of the ground situation, organizations spend excessive time, money and effort to achieve their goals.

Breaking the silo mindset to reduce the impact of executive isolation doesn't happen merely by coaching and advising managers; most managers listen to the advice but do not actually implement it. Organizations need very clear executable strategies to re-orient divisions towards collaborating for the growth of the company.

INFUSE FLEXIBILITY NOT BREAKDOWNS

Cross-functional teamwork is a must for delivery of complex projects across teams and locations. Here, one doesn't always need to blame structures and silos. In silos, transferrable skills are seldom developed since everyone just aligns to the requirements of the specific department. Making two differently skilled professionals work alongside one another doesn't lead to cross pollination of skills—would an artist magically learn engineering skills if made to sit next to an engineer while working? Similarly, it is not imaginable that the head of security will be entrusted with deciphering complex numbers and excel sheets in a business management meeting. Hence, structures and silos don't have to be damned at the time. All it needs is to ensure that people from cross-functional units are able to work together, based on their skill sets and cognitive abilities, to achieve collective goals. Collaborative effort of different teams can result in figuring out multiple ways of solving a problem, by challenging and questioning each other in a constructive manner. Breaking down silos begins with earning mutual respect, which further leads to collaboration and reduced executive isolation. Encouraging regular meetings between cross-functional team members helps in developing engaging dialogue. This allows better execution of the collective vision by the specialist divisions.

MAKE THE MISSION MORE CRITICAL THAN THE PROCESS

Cultivating a culture that conveys that the mission of the team is more important than the unit or the division they represent, is an effective way to reduce silo-based practices. Like in the Indian movie *Chak De India*, the coach made every player believe that they represent the country and not respective geographical states. They eventually become a solid team winning the coveted medals. How many times, during the course of our employment, do we hear 'I know it's important, but my process doesn't permit the action'? One tends to forget that the commitment of an organization to its clients and shareholders is what makes its reputation. The processes can always be aligned and relooked at to ensure that the organization's commitments to its stakeholders are always fulfilled. It is quite possible that individual divisions developed the processes and standard operating procedures. When large teams work on complex processes, divisions are not singled out to own success or failure. Ownership of outcomes should be encouraged on the whole. When the senior leadership shares the project vision in time with subordinate managers and teams, they get a buy in to be a part of the battle. Then comes the delegation of authority (not tasks per se), to empower the managers and their teams by giving the flexibility to figuring out the best way of accomplishing mission critical assignments.

A COMMUNICATIONS POLICY THAT WORKS

Townhalls, open-houses, emails, skip-level meetings—effectively every such instrument is an opportunity to communicate. This can happen either virtually or in person. On top of that there are chat and collaboration tools available for transactional conversations. However, having the necessary tools and actually being able to really communicate may not be the same thing. Problems and challenges are seldom communicated fast enough to the relevant stakeholders, in spite of all kinds of communication mediums being available. Many a times it's a confusing communication policy that comes in the way of people from all divisions knowing about something critical that requires immediate addressal.

For example, teams know that for a problem needing a resolution within 24 hours, there is a dashboard available on which such uncertain situations can be posted. This helps the teams to qualify whether the issue at hand is operational/transactional or critical enough to be brought to management attention. Qualifying the severity of the issue helps the management time to not be spent on trivial matters and they don't get loaded with unnecessary problems. Guidelines for when to use different types of communication methods available, like emails, phonecalls, can be specified for some critical projects. More than the quantum of communication, the cross-functional work efficacy depends on the actions taken on the communication: more the actions, lesser the silos and isolation.

EXECUTIVE ISOLATION BY DIGITAL TRANSFORMATIONS

More than the nature and frequency of communication, the cross-functional work efficacy depends on the actions taken based on communication between team members and the management. More actions mean less silo development and isolation. Many organizations integrate the use of social networking tools like LinkedIn, Facebook and technology enabled platforms like Telegram and Slack in their work and communication flow. These were expected to make humans more connected, reachable and efficient. However, it seems that digital transformation also enhances the case and impact of executive isolation.

In a 2009 survey done by InterNations, it was found that 25 per cent of people who took expatriate assignments wanted to leave their cushy, rewarding international assignment quite early—the most common reason being cited was loneliness. Thirty per cent of the respondents expected their firms to provide them with frequent professional networking services and opportunities.

Consider what most social and professional interaction platforms have to offer—Facebook claims it 'gives people the power to share, and make the world a more open and connected place'; similarly LinkedIn's mission is to 'Connect the world's professionals to make them more productive and successful'; Slack proudly calls itself a 'collaboration hub' that helps organizations to connect its teams and unify its communication systems. However, all the tools being deployed for collaboration are reducing meaningful in-person interactions. Since, middle managers and teams prefer not to virtually communicate day-to-day progress or problems with the CXOs to avoid oversharing, this combined with the lack of in-person interaction, also contributes to executive isolation.

Most of the CXOs start spending considerable time to polish their online profiles and keep them updated. Some do for reputation management and others to maybe figure out in a job search. However, if CXOs spend excessive time on digital networking, it eats into the time they might have allocated for personal interactions with frontline teams and subordinate managers. Somehow, the posts on LinkedIn start getting associated with the intelligence of a managerial personnel. Similarly, higher-level managers are expected to write on the company intranet about success stories and losses/wins case analyses. CXOs must divert time from keeping up with digital media to ensure they don't forget to give enough time to motivating employees.

Further, the digital collaboration tools and remote working results in working extra-time and also poses a time-zone conflict. While executive isolation starts at work, the ability to work from anywhere and anytime eats into a person's personal life as well. Eventually it starts to eat into quality time with friends and family as well.

THE UPSHOT

No single skill can ever fill the requirements of an organization. Subordinate managers need the spotlight and need to feel valued but not at the expense of personal agendas and isolating their bosses. This requires maintaining a transparent culture and develop policies and practices to keep communication channels between different levels of employees, open, in a well-structured manner. Different divisions in a company collaborate when there is reciprocation and viability of time, once the missions are aligned. Executive isolation and silo situations are mindset issues more than a way of working. Once the middle managers know that and appreciate the advantages of keeping communication channels between them and their bosses as well as their teams, open, they can achieve healthy cooperation and collaboration.

When I was employed at Avaya, a copy of my letter of incentives was sent to my mother instead of being handed over to me. It had a far-reaching impact on my respect for the organization and the leadership. The leadership connected with the employees at a deeper level and significantly enhanced the interactions. The battle to avoid executive isolation is to ensure spending time in building connections. With a generous approach and sense of gratitude, one can build meaningful connections to overcome loneliness and isolation.

As a practice, during her tenure as the CEO of PepsiCo, it is said that Indra Nooyi wrote many letters to the parents of the senior executives in her company. The intent was to inform the parents how their children are an asset for the company, and everyone is proud of their contributions. It was a simple yet effective act of gratitude that developed strong connections between Indira and her teams. Due to the effective culture embedded with compassion and gratitude at the workplace, she would have felt less isolated and more involved than peer CXOs in other companies of similar scale and operations. When middle managers are being developed and coached for senior levels, they must also be mentored to seek out and mitigate signs of practices that may lead to executive isolation as they progress in the career. One of the core leadership missions must be to cultivate meaningful connections. The ability to develop meaningful connections reduces executive isolation and fosters a culture of inclusiveness.

Success and sense of achievement is always a result of team effort. Successful leaders keep reinforcing the positive connections at the workplace; it acts as a glue to hold the network together and achieve desired objectives. Everyone desires to feel engaged, acknowledged and invested in their own and company's interests.

Forming connection with the organization, its employees and stakeholders is the tool to effectively combat executive isolation.

FURTHER READINGS

Dalla-Camina, Megan. 2018. 'The Reality of Imposter Syndrome.' https://www.psychologytoday.com/us/blog/real-women/201809/the-reality-imposter-syndrome

Jonsson, Nick. 2019. 'Is Digital Transformation Increasing Executive Isolation.' https://www.peoplemattersglobal.com/blog/life-at-work/is-digital-transformation-increasing-executive-isolation-23757

Meagher, Kieron, and Andrew Wait. 2015. 'Trust, Credibility and Delegation: Evidence from Multiple Employees per Establishment.' Available at SSRN: https://ssrn.com/abstract=2558840 or http://dx.doi.org/10.2139/ssrn.2558840

Umah, Ruth. 2018. 'PepsiCo CEO Indra Nooyi: 5 Powerful Career Habits that Drove Her Success.' https://www.cnbc.com/2018/10/02/pepsico-ceo-indra-nooyis-last-day-5-habits-that-drove-her-success.html

TRADING RELATIONSHIPS WITH RESULTS: ATTACHMENT INHIBITING DETACHMENT

As a manager and a leader, there are many existential issues we face: When to let go? What to embrace?

Many skip managers tend to carry the baggage of relationships with the teams they managed over the course of their careers. Despite having a middle manager to manage the teams, such skip managers keep dragging their feet on handing over the management of team members, who are no longer their direct reportees, to the new middle manager. Many skip managers keep practising traditional command-and-control approaches to keep managing the people who are now two levels below them. It's called Obsession with Leadership that stems from the social and cultural management elements related to the management group norms, shared values and perceptions and mutual consensus related to goals and objectives. An existing manager who has aligned his team to these nuances is not able to let go of the team even on becoming their skip manager. Such managers are obsessed with their team and continue to press upon their ways of problem-solving.

In 2014, Kieron J. Meagher and Andrew Wait published a research article titled *Evidence from Multiple Employees per Establishment on Trust, Credibility and Delegation*, in which they examined the examined the degree of trust that employees have on the management to facilitate uninterrupted working, and the delegation of decision-making authority at various managerial levels. When I was working for an Indian multinational company, my team and I always had certain conflicts with the production department about timely supply of equipment based on the delivery dates committed by the sales team. We had a specific point of contact at the factory; whenever we complained about the delay, he always tried to stall by stating one of the following excuses: When we make a deal with a new vendor to save time and costs, we need to make a long proposal, and forecast the outcomes with the new vendor over three years, which takes time; then we give that to the senior management and have to wait till it is addressed by the management; this also takes time because of the many other priorities of the CEO. As a result, most of the times, the delay in approval cost us parts of contracts.

Later in my career, I worked in a company where the functions were decentralized; however, this came with its own set of problems—the staff worked quickly or sluggishly based on their preference to support certain managers in certain geographies. While the manager in production had the authority to decide on what value of deal needs to be prioritized over the other, he didn't have the acumen to understand which country's business unit needed the material/equipment first. So, if a manager personally known to him would call and insist on material allocation, chances are he will be given priority. There was a conflicting balance of power with relationships that might be causing the organization more harm than good. An organization's success depends on (a) how delegation and decentralization of work across locations affect people's trust in the organization and (b) the relationship of skip managers with the individuals reporting to the middle or his/her subordinate managers. One of my acquaintances, Harry, worked in the fashion accessories segment and was involved in two specific product launch marketing projects related to the same product category—sunglasses. The industry was going through a paradigm shift where the retailing of sunglasses had a new competitor channel—online sales. The introduction of this new channel of sale brought immense changes in the ways of marketing sunglasses. For generations, people liked to go to a store, try out various looks and make a purchase. But with the launch of online stores that gave a 360 degrees 3-D view of the face with virtual sunglasses, a major chunk of the young generation started shifting to virtual shopping for purchasing sunglasses.

Harry was deployed in a team that was developing the marketing collaterals for the sunglasses and they had recently been assigned a new manager. The old manager had been promoted to the skip level and the new reporting manager leading their team was a lateral hire from the industry. In the course of developing the marketing collaterals for both the projects, the skip manager was slightly more involved in one project than the other. Incidentally the skip manager gave much more support and favourable reviews for the marketing material created for the project he was more immersed in. For this project, the skip manager even ruled over certain marketing decisions taken by the subordinate manager. As for the project in which the skip manager was not involved, he just used some traditional evaluation metrics to give a go/no go to the marketing material made for the campaign. It seemed that the skip manager was not able to detach himself from his former team, i.e., the team that handled the former project, and was unable to pass on the reigns to the new middle manager. This cognitive behaviour of giving favouring decisions in cases where a manager is more involved in a process can lead to biased outcomes and maintain relationships may be given precedence to getting results. As conveyed by Harry, due to the closer supervision of the project by the skip manager, the marketing collaterals were less creative and impactful, proving that imagination needs a free run and not a framework.

Skip managers want that the number of employees in their team should keep growing. This gives the skip managers a sense of rising control as they have more people to delegate the work to in a decentralized working culture. Eventually the skip manager is neither able to provide constructive direction to the subordinate managers, nor to the former team he is still trying to control, leading to the output being compromised. Skip managers tend to overvalue the work done by teams they supervise as compared to the work performed by the team that is more closely associated with the subordinate managers.

The ideal way for a skip manager to work is to get involved when asked and not by forcing his supervision on team that need to learn how to work with the new manager. Efficient organization structures and team engagement cultures don't confuse individual contributors by exposing them to parallel authorities.

APPROPRIATE SOCIAL SKILLS FOR THE WORKPLACE

In a new-age workplace, socializing between peers, subordinates or members of other workgroups is important. It can be virtual for remote teams or in-person when the teams are in the vicinity. With so many people working in close quarters, strained social interactions are unavoidable and when that happens, it leads to failed outcomes, burnouts and unfriendly, unacceptable public altercations. More often than not, employees call on their reporting managers when things go out of hand, however, once in a while they may reach out to the skip manager who used to be their reporting manager. It is possible that a resilient attitude may make some employees thrive despite strained interactions at the workplace. However, if such episodes are allowed to continue, they lead to mistrust and, eventually, can negatively influence collaboration and cooperation between colleagues.

Handling Relationships: From Scott Butcher's Experiences

Scott Butcher is a Stanford LEAD alumnus working out of San Francisco, USA. He shared a very interesting experience with me about relationships at work.

Bruce Kiddoo was the CFO of Maxim Integrated for 12 years until his retirement in October 2019. The company had recently implemented a new SAP ERP system and was focused on improving their reputation after a stock option restatement. Bruce was hired in 2007 in the wake of a stock option probe that had led to the resignation of the former CFO, to rebuild the company reputation. He made a wonderful CFO, beloved by employees, deeply involved in employee development, showed integrity and focused on scalable and efficient operations. He was incredibly successful in growing Maxim's earnings per share through cost-saving initiatives. Scott left PricewaterhouseCoopers to start work at Maxim Integrated in 2010 in the company's brand-new Internal Audit department. After the managing director of the department, Scott was the first person hired by the company for this department. Bruce became Scott's mentor during his seven years at Maxim and he will never forget how much of an impact Bruce had on his growth and development. Scott shares three things about their relationship, which I believe will benefit the readers of this book.

First, Scott took the initiative to ask Bruce to meet with him despite only being a manager in the organization. He approached Bruce and asked him for a one-on-one meeting to discuss a new role in the Accounting department. Scott indicated that he wanted to get Bruce's thoughts on the new role, understand the pros and cons of hiring for the role and how he could produce the most value for the organization. Bruce was intrigued by Scott's proactiveness and with time became interested in Scott's personal and professional development. After their first meeting, they continued the one-on-one sessions during Scott's time at Maxim; Bruce became one of his best mentors.

Second, Bruce became a champion and advocate for Scott as a result of their meetings together. He helped ensure that Scott was successful in each of his department rotations, namely, Accounting and Procurement. Scott realized an amazing amount of success as a result of Bruce's executive support. Bruce was always ready to create opportunities, offer guidance and provide resources to Scott. In the Accounting department, Bruce's role involved transforming global systems and processes in accounting. Bruce helped to ensure that Scott had weekly meetings with his direct report VPs and directors. During these meetings Scott gave project updates, key result areas, communicated expected roadblocks and shared relevant action items. In the Procurement department, Bruce provided Scott with developers, business system analysts, procurement resources and other resources in order to implement new procurement systems, achieve cost saving goals, transform processes and implement new processes and integrate the process and functions of newly acquired companies.

Third, Bruce was deeply involved in each of these departments through budget reviews, goal setting, project updates and metric reporting. He also did something really different from other CFOs, which was to host offsites with other skip managers and employees of each of the departments. The notable absentees were the directors of the departments. During these meetings, each staff member could openly discuss their personal and departmental challenges, pain points, opportunities and concerns. The result of these meetings with staff members was that Bruce was able to understand how the team was really performing. Bruce learned a lot and he implemented action plans/new projects to address departmental issues and opportunities. As per Scott, he had never seen a CFO so proactive to ensure that each individual department as well as the entire organization is successful.

In the above context, was there also an undercurrent which might have been overlooked? Imagine if Scott's manager was not at all comfortable with this parallel authority and camaraderie between Scott and Bruce? Things turned out well for them, however, for some, it could have strained certain professional relationships.

Interpersonal relationships at work between employees at different hierarchical levels depend on the quality and magnitude of attachment. Depending on the type and severity of the attachment issues, the skip managers may demonstrate lack of self-esteem, jittery and impulsive behaviour and low empathy for subordinate managers. Certain skip managers are not able to let go of their former teams since some of the team members were used as emotional dumping grounds. This affects the team members also since they find the managerial transition more difficult than others and are not able to align well with the immediate managers. This becomes worse if the skip managers continue to discuss their personal and emotional problems with them during informal, social settings. The attachment of managers to their reportees has a direct impact on the burnout rate of the teams, whether the subordinate manager realizes this or not. Social and professional interactions between various hierarchical levels at the workplace are supposed to act as stress busters, however, more often than not these outings become exhaustive and sometimes abusive. The teams continue to feel victimized, caught between a war of control between the immediate and skip manager.

Everyone in an organization is a part of the attachment theory. Essentially, the theory explains how individuals at the workplace respond to and cope with situations arising out of interpersonal relations including but not limited to parallel authorities. The theory delves into the behavioural aspects of excessive attachment or detachment between professionals. Every person at work has an attachment pattern that might stem from their personal living patterns. A dysfunctional attachment pattern can lead to conflicting issues between employees at different levels. The quantity issues may increase when the teams start to grow in number.

On the other hand, employees who get consistent support, care and guidance from a manager at work tend to develop a secure attachment style. Professionals that are securely attached are able to develop effective working models for themselves, which help them when engaging with others. They demonstrate comfort in relationships with high self-efficacy if faced with uncertain and stressful situations at the workplace. However, this secure attachment may become toxic when, eventually, that manager moves up the ranks, and he/she is unable to let go of their attachment with team; such managers may start to demonstrate inconsistent behaviour as skip managers. Overall, it leads to challenges for everyone including the individual contributors in the team, the reporting manager and the skip manager.

The skip managers tend to become hypersensitive and develop a compelling need to be close to their former teams with whom he/she enjoyed a secure attachment. Lack of such opportunities leads to internal and external conflicts for the skip managers and eventually impacts professional and business results and outcomes.

Subordinate managers end up being less bothered about the work and business outcomes and feel more anxious about being rejected by their reportees, co-workers and their managers. It leads to them demonstrating withdrawal and isolation symptoms while dealing with the anxiety of being accepted by their colleagues, more than the need to achieve results. The level of professional emotional attachment at the workplace directly impacts the quantum of participation that the employee offers to contribute in achieving organizational goals.

TRUST ISSUES AND BURNOUTS

Trust is defined as the extent to which one professional will have confidence in the good intentions, words and actions of other professionals at the workplace. The level of trust demonstrated between all the hierarchical levels—individual contributors, their managers and skip managers—in a cohesive team context, is expected to demonstrate better performance and greater ideation in innovation.

It seems that the impact of uncertain authority and the interactions with managers and skip managers has the highest effect on the morale of new joinees. As employees spend more time in the organization, they understand the culture better and develop improved level of psychological safety. This also rubs off on the team members during team interactions. The employees' relationship with colleagues and supervisors ensures trust or the lack of it. Eventually teams that are caught in the crossfire between parallel authorities and attachment issues with supervisors at various levels start to demonstrate chronic exhaustion. This is a sign of burnouts, which are then followed by emotional distancing from work. Nature of supervisory relationships have a direct link to the strained quality of output due to potential burnouts and exhaustion. In the absence of trusting relationships between various levels, it becomes hard to share the credit for the team's accomplishments, which leads to a battle for claiming the credit. When managers at different hierarchical levels develop a great sense of belonging for their team members, in socially as well as towards the organization's objectives, the burnouts are less, imparting a sense of well-being.

THE FLIPSIDE OF RELATIONSHIPS AT THE WORKPLACE

It is natural to have friendly relations at the workplace due to the amount of time spent in office. However, one has to consider the downside of such relationships turning into more than casual, specially relationships between different hierarchical levels. In an organization, you can't choose your peers and projects; most of the times the managers decide both. On one hand there are organizations with strict multi-level hierarchical structures, while on the other hand companies like Google promote a buddy culture, encouraging friendly relations between co-workers at different hierarchical levels. In such a social culture, the younger generation of professionals become informal quite fast and may start blurring the lines between personal and professional lives.

There is a new phrase that has become increasingly used at the workplace—*bring your life to office*, implying that social bonds can supersede professional engagements when authentic self-disclosures and initiatives become the key to better performance. However, this may make things more complex as well.

A friendly, informal relationship with managers can initially feel amazing due to the thought that friendliness will be the key to productivity and engagement. However, little do employees acknowledge the downside of such scenarios.

Informality and friendliness beyond a certain level can lead to emotional distractions and conflict between one's role as a manager and as a friend. If there were 10 people in a team and one of them is promoted to supervise the team, he/she may not be able to impose requisite control and intervention, simply because till yesterday he/she was friends with the nine reportees. Due to certain amount of tensions between the new manager and the team, there tends to be reduced communication leading to silo formation. Eventually it can lead to the manager developing a better rapport with few of the reportees who become favourites and such favouritism gets exhibited while assigning tasks. If managers and subordinates become friends rather than being friendly, it starts to reflect on the way the team is handled and eventually on the results for the organization. A manager can always reprimand a friendly team member but may find it difficult reprimanding a 'friend' at the workplace.

This is indicative of the Goldilocks Effect. When it comes to adapting oneself in a new team at workplace or at a new job, if something is too familiar, people get turned off and lack of familiarity can lead to scepticism. So, everyone tries to find their comfort zone and align the teams and managers accordingly. This is further complicated by the social media where one needs to maintain the façade on personal life in line with the perceptions built at the workplace.

So, how should managers, skips and teams approach 'attachment' at the workplace to avoid its downsides?

Overall, some amount of attachment with people at work can be a wonderful and enriching experience. It may be necessary to bond to a certain extent in order to get things done. Skip managers try to maintain their bonds with their former teams. When the bonds are healthy, they can help the skip managers to keep themselves aware of the happenings on the battlefield, without indulging loose talkers and whistle-blowers. There are policies that managers, both middle and skip, institute in order to manage the framework of attachment like regulating the frequency of formal lunches with the team, other divisions or managers. This is to indicate that the organization wants to set a limit on the informal connections between people at the workplace. Over-attachment with certain employees may lead to the phenomenon of teacher's pet, in which other employees begin to perceive the attachment as favouritism for some and unfairness for others. Once the 'attachment' between the manager and subordinates becomes stronger, the thin line between ability to recognize someone for performance or giving recognition due to favouritism, begins to blur. Hence, at every level, employees must be cognizant of maintaining boundaries. If managers focus their attention on only a few employees and offer them high visibility projects, they tend to overlook growth opportunities and skill sets of others that can actually fast track projects. If the teams start believing that the measure of success is not performance based but the basis is the personal attachment with the manager, a war of attention ensues rather than delivery of objectives.

Managing a Versatile Team: The Personal Angle

Juana-Catalina Rodriguez lives in France. She is a specialist in innovation, strategy and marketing. She has gained invaluable work experience in the last 20 years, creating value for different industries. She can be defined as a serial entrepreneur and strategic leader with international experience in the B2C and B2B marketplaces in sectors such as financial services, fast-moving consumer goods, cloud storage, mobile services, digital identities and digital transformation. Juana is also a Stanford LEAD alumnus and has led cross-functional project teams across different regions.

According to her the fundamental challenges of balancing attachment and delivering business results has a starting point in striving to keep all the team members equally motivated, directly affecting productivity. Throughout human history, trust has been a key asset for any relationship. She quotes the Oxford Dictionary definition of trust: Trust is the firm belief in the reliability, truth or ability of someone or something; for example, 'I trust you because you are reliable.' When the team gets bigger it is not an easy task creating this reliable relationship with each team member.

She further asserts that developing a strong collaborative structure is not as easy when teams become bigger due to globalization and virtual working, thanks to technology. Developing strong links in teams over 10–20 people is a challenge. It requires a lot of effort from managers and executive leaders, especially when the teams have highly skilled people. It takes effort to not demonstrate any favouritism. As an example, she says that when there are around 50 attendees for a two-hour call, not everyone would get the chance to relay their point of view. However, if during every such call only few of the same set of people are able to talk, that is when the calls become an exercise in futility. The pertinent question is whether this can lead to the perception that some employees are more thorough than others? Another critical aspect of collaboration as per Juana is that when teams get bigger and start operating virtually, the aspect of reliance on human networking becomes much more critical. Even if today we have a lot of tools, like Slack, Microsoft Teams or Workplace to connect, these tools only work when the culture of collaboration and trust is inherently present in the team. These tools are potentially effective when the teammates have a feeling of being provided equal opportunities to contribute to and deliver important projects.

She also believes that attachment with teams has something to do with people preventing access to the managerial levels above. One person friendly with the higher managerial level will try to shield that layer so that it's not penetrated by anyone else. People who keep their managers isolated are afraid of losing their authority or legitimacy within the system.

She had a great mentor within the company she was working for at the time; he was in charge of a business unit and offered Juana the opportunity to join one of his teams. One of his direct reportees became her boss. Juana's new boss was a control freak; he wanted to know and follow everything and be sure his boss, the senior VP, believed that everything was under control. He applied an old-fashioned management style, including micromanagement.

After a few exchanges with her boss, Juana was told that that she wasn't allowed to speak with the senior VP as he was the only one who could have access to him. He explained to her that he didn't want to give his boss access to the day-to-day working of the team. This served a double purpose since he also wanted to keep his team isolated from his boss, so that he continues to be the boss's favourite and avoids any of the other team members getting close to the boss. Juana believes that she learned a good lesson of leadership from this experience as her manager was certainly afraid of losing his favourable status and was unhealthily concerned about what everyone else thought about him as a manager. He felt so insecure that the idea of his team speaking with the boss directly, worried him; he felt the team would make him look foolish or result in his losing control of the team. This kind of behaviour is very specific to certain insecure mangers, but as long as a team is founded on trust and open communication and managers are self-confident, the scenario of executive isolation won't arise.

Juana also realized that some skip-level executives that are very immersive, don't let their subordinate managers do their job. They keep trying to control everything and interact directly with the manager's team, that might have been reporting to the skip manager formerly.

Juana believes that the effect of managers getting friendly with the teams depends on the managers and the organizational culture. Being friendly doesn't mean not being professional and ignoring if the team members are not performing their tasks to obtain results. While being friendly with people at the workplace may not be a problem, it always gets discussed at length at organizations where relationships and office politics get mixed.

Juana has worked in different countries and has been exposed to numerous cultures; she acknowledges that being friendly can contribute to the firm foundation of a team. After becoming a skip manager, one doesn't need to stop being friendly with the teams. But drawing some boundaries in line with the requirements of the new status quo to avoid confusion is more important. Sometimes the skip managers address the teams to reinforce a certain message in the interest of the organization. However, if the subordinate manager is not aligned with the skip manager, it creates confusion in the team regarding their goals and expected outcomes. This is when the problem of parallel authorities arises, which leads to tension in the teams, since most employees end up following the higher authority.

Juana believes that it's important to emphasize the importance of trust, resilience, confidence and clarity in managing a team. The best results she got came from teams that became a 'family' with a common and clear purpose. Together they mourned mistakes and celebrated wins and they all knew the opportunities and challenges that lay ahead of them.

THE INTERPLAY OF CONFIDENCE AND RISK

Confidence is a very important characteristic in a manager. If the team sees the leader hesitating, it creates confusion and they lose hope. The leader must be ready to take risks aligned with his beliefs. Clarity, purpose and priorities must be clear, reinforced and objectified for everyone in the team. The worst a manager can see is a team that does not have direction and just keep on working on a to-do list every day. In this case, some employees are able to take credit of other's work. To be an unbiased leader, one needs to empathize with people, needs to understand their motivations to be able to drive them out of the comfort zone and needs to be willing to run the extra mile with the team.

If you are part of a team that is being managed by a former manager who is now a skip manager and you have a close relationship with the skip manager, chances are that being a favourite of an earlier manager make the new manager resentful toward you. There is no upside to attachment at work leading to favouritism. If your colleagues and your reporting manager get a feeling that you are being singled out as a favourite of the boss's boss, and have progressed in the ranks purely due to such favouritism, they will resent it and become unsupportive. So, it's in your interests to initiate a discussion with the skip manager about playing down the attachment. If the situation is not actively corrected by you, the struggle to fulfil the aspirations of parallel authorities will eventually start compromising your own performance. If the opportunities you got were based on merit, but others perceive them as a result of favouritism, the new manager will begin undermining your passion and hard work. Do ensure to keep the relevant HR manager informed about favouritism at the workplace so that any recourse or corrective measures are on the record.

Let the earlier managers understand that while they have got higher ranks and more resources, your regular day is still packed with a lot of tasks that demand time and that hasn't changed for you. It's important to keep the engagement with earlier bosses as professional as possible. The job is not to entertain or amuse the bosses in order to befriend them. If a person is seen as going over the head of the reporting manager to become friendly with the skip managers, he or she endangers the cooperation he can get from peers when it's needed the most. No one would like to be ostracized by their current team and manager at the expense of trying to be friendly with former managers. Such endeavours and initiatives lead to short-term success. Also, the first casualty of being branded as 'attached to a skip manager' is the loss of trust of peers and the immediate manager. Skip managers, who are not able to let go of their attachment with some people are responsible for jeopardizing those people's careers. The new teams and managers tend to doubt the sincerity and trustworthiness of anyone considered as a teacher's pet. It is only together that the skip managers, subordinate managers and teams can create a professional level playing field for everyone to get equal opportunities to perform, learn and get rewarded.

The amount of attachment at the workplace is high if people have abandonment issues and don't want to be working in isolation. The other end of the spectrum is avoidance, a situation in which people don't want anyone to know about their personality and habits beyond office hours. Professionals with a strong sense of security have positive internal working, which implies they will be calm, composed and would be approached by others just to get a positive feeling, when the morale is down. Such professionals handle stress well and believe that they can ask for support when needed and in turn offer their support to anyone who asks. This attitude also reflects in their physical and mental health.

Employees and managers who fear abandonment at the workplace have very high levels of anxiety and keep on doubting their potential. As a result, they develop a negative view about themself and keep finding themselves in a spate of self-blame. Such people are edgy while conversing with people in meetings and otherwise, and in order to avoid feeling left out or rejected, they might continue interfering in others work due to a compulsive urge to be close to a group. Since they have a negative view about themselves, as managers, such people become overbearing on their reportees and continue to be overbearing even when they no longer supervise them. In order to not feel rejected at the workplace such individuals start avoiding conflicts and at times give approvals for things they should not approve.

On the flipside are professionals who have a negative view about other people at the workplace. Such managers don't like to delegate and always have trust issues with others. They prefer to be self-reliant, don't want to depend on others and don't want anyone to depend on them. If promoted to managerial ranks, these people have a tendency to create trust issues and hence are better as individual contributors. These managers have a closed-door-seek-appointment policy with their teams and prefer to keep emotional distance from others. They possibly don't experience supportive environment on the work floor and that can impact outcomes based on how teams react to such managerial practices.

STUCK IN A POINT OF VIEW

A stronghold happens when managers or peers have complete disregard for what others think about an important work situation at hand. At this stage, if the manager has risen up the ranks to a skip position, he/she may even tend to disregard the middle manager and directly start commenting and rejecting the opinions of the team members if they have worked together earlier. The managers tend to stick to their own point of views and fail to hear what the middle manager or the team members have to say. The reason for such a tendency is the preconceived notion that the manager is always right. In such situations, communication becomes heavy-handed and the team members feel like a child being parented by their managers. Skip managers should not keep taking their previous teams for granted and ignoring their views just because he knows the team for a longer duration than their new manager. When skip managers keep ignoring the middle managers to dictate the teams below, their professional relationship gets compromised with both the levels, the manager as well as the team under him.

MAKING UP MATTERS

Ever heard of the concept of fake fast tracking by dropping names? An example of this would be 'the CEO might need this report by tomorrow'. This is a classic manoeuvre of making up a situation that doesn't exist and may never happen. However just to make the team work faster, managers tend to scare them into finishing the work by mentioning that the CXOs expect it to be done. The team starts to feel they will be disappointing the leadership if the work is not done within a certain time frame, which is made up by the reporting manager in the first place and such a demand doesn't actually exist. The new managers initially try this trick and if the team takes the bait, then name dropping to fast track work becomes a habit. Eventually, the team starts to feel burned out and the results start to get compromised. In order to develop an honest relationship with the teams, managers should let them know that it is you who wants the work to be completed by a certain time. This way the teams don't consider the manager to be a messenger and truly try to develop trust and deliver results.

ATTACHING ATTRIBUTES

Peter was a very effective and aggressive manager, working in a telecom company. He got promoted and the organization hired a new manager, Jason to take his place. In the new scheme of things, Peter became Jason's manager and Peter's earlier team started reporting to Jason. Being new in the organization, Jason insisted that Peter joins the first team meeting being hosted by Jason and share few thoughts about the work ahead. This idea turned into a disaster. Peter was still not leaving his old team mentally. So, when the meeting started, the team was all happy that they have a new manager Jason and Peter as a skip will have their back. However, Peter sat with his cup of coffee and said, 'Folks I guess you would get time to know Jason well and likewise he would get to know you. But I will spare him some trouble and at least tell him a bit about you all.' Thereafter, everyone was hit with an unbelievable flurry of negative attributes getting attached to few of the team members. 'You know Jason,' said Peter, 'here is your best performer, Dane, but he can really be mean and selfish you know.' Dane smiles thinking this was just a casual remark, however, Peter reinforced, 'No, this is really the truth, Jason. Dane can really be difficult at times.' Jason didn't react but realized calling Peter to the meeting was a mistake since it was evident that Peter was acting out as he was not happy to let go of his old team. Peter, meanwhile, was operating from a different state of mind and labelled every team member with one negative attribute or the other. As a result, Jason and the team started their engagement on a very uncomfortable note Instead of an inclusive meeting, Jason could have asked for a one-on-one meeting with Peter and taken feedback about the team members in confidence rather than letting Peter get under their skin.

It is possible to reduce the impact of relationships over results by avoiding crossover connections and avoiding constant criticism from the senior personnel. Improving personal and professional communication and being mindful of the channels for giving and receiving information are important steps to balance attachment and results.

FURTHER READINGS

Clay, Kelly. 2013. 'The Goldilocks Effect: Why Silicon Valley Is No Longer "Just Right".' https://www.forbes.com/sites/kellyclay/2013/07/30/the-goldilocks-effect-why-silicon-valley-is-no-longer-just-right/#152df16e68ae

BUILDING TRUST: EFFECTIVE MOTIVATION

Psychological safety in the workplace is felt when managers and peers do not penalize a person or think they are not good enough, just because of a mistake made by them. In an environment that is considered psychologically safe, people don't mock others or appear as showstoppers, creating hurdles for the ones asking for help, feedback or information, to slow them down. In a safe culture, asking questions without a fear of retribution is acceptable and welcomed, which leads to confident teams that can take risks for a better future of the company.

In today's world, driven by technology and uncertainty, a major part of organizations' success depends a psychologically safe atmosphere, ensured by the managerial personnel. It is important for managers to create a culture of psychological safety for their teams.

When beginning to develop and manage large teams, the leaders must be able to foster open communication and conversations that can promote mutual engagement and enhance levels of cognitive safety in the organization at large.

In the absence of the culture of questioning and cognitive resilience, employees tend to consider peer and managerial pressure to be more than a transactional issue at work. They start viewing these situations as a threat to their position at the company. In turn the team starts to focus on the negative consequences of not obeying their managers. This results in lack of creative thought, as the employees are fearful of developing thinking practices of innovation and bringing new ideas on the table.

As the team starts to grow in number, it is important to develop a culture that looks beyond competence of the team members. The managers need to buckle up and put robust practices in place including regular feedback, development of effective relations, setting a proper incentive structure and development of a supportive work environment. Without these elements, the teams tend to lack the attitude for high performance and collaboration. A positive mental and emotional state psyche is conducive to developing trust and a sense of belonging in the organization. The role of managers at this juncture is to inspire the teams to be resilient and motivated.

While CXOs and venture founders develop the strategy and direction of the company, the groundwork has to be done by the skip and subordinate managers. Team members look up to their immediate and skip managers rather than the CXOs for psychological and cognitive security. When the teams feel that their managers have made the workplace psychologically safe, it leads to better collaboration and performance. Such a culture is not just good for business but also good for the employee's health and morale.

Vijaya Vardhan Panthagani is a Stanford LEAD alumnus with close to two decades of corporate experience. He believes there are multiple dynamics at play at all managerial levels, which can impact the interactions between them.

As per him, human psychology is exactly what it is—human. A cocktail of hormones and emotions has been brewing within human beings since the dawn of evolution. The basic ingredients are the need to feel valued, accepted and appreciated for who we intrinsically are. However, people at all levels in the workplace, whether the ones managing, or the ones being managed, need a psychologically safe environment.

Both psychological and environmental safety are powerful feelings that drive people's behaviour in a variety of settings, especially in a strict hierarchical organization. As we go higher up the corporate ladder, we become associated with power, prestige and privileges. Whether we like to capitalize on it or not is a whole different argument.

Vijaya recounted the story of a colleague who was a manager at one of the company's Vijaya worked at, also as a manager. For the sake of anonymity, he would prefer to call him JV. JV was an extrovert and a masterful relationship builder. He came across as a friendly, helpful and an influential individual. His direct reportees loved him. Peers enjoyed his presence. Bosses felt he was the employee experience guy, who treated employees as though they were stakeholders and needed an adaptable and fulfilling workplace to have a productive, engaged and effective staff. A year later his reporting changed from one director to another. Making no mistake, using his influence and relationship building skills, he quickly got into the good books of the new director as well. He was still working on an employee engagement project, which was initiated when he was reporting to his former boss and the new boss allowed him to continue working on the same. Skip engagements were ongoing while JV was excited and motivated about the innovative projects in hand. One fine day, JV walked into his former boss's office to get his opinion on a budget decision for the project during the upcoming year. They chatted as usual and JV left his former boss's office satisfied with the discussion. Now was there something strange in this?

Within days JV noticed that his new boss was acting aloof with him. JV was left out of a few important meetings of which he should have been a part. Moreover, the new boss also reduced the frequency of his one-on-one meetings with JV and JV's promotion that was due did not happen. He had to wait for a full six months before it came to pass. JV's goodwill and psychological safety was under question; he wondered if there had been any miscommunication between him and the manager when he realized that his former and current bosses were good friends. They obviously talked about him between themselves. JV realized that the new boss was offended when JV went to the former boss for the budget discussion and wanted to punish JV for it. Poor JV had no inkling that such an innocent discussion would hurt his development at the company. Once he came to know through the grapevine what had happened, he immediately switched into overdrive to salvage his relationship with his new boss. This was perceived as 'sucking up or schmoozing' by his new boss and when his next promotion opportunity came, the message JV got from the boss was clear—'I don't have an issue with you staying here as you are not harmful, but you are going to stay where you are as long as you work here.' The point here was that JV's boss's ego had been hurt and his primal desire to be respected had been affected. This episode is reminiscent of the saying, 'Don't ruffle the feathers of an eagle, the bite can be fatal.' We can argue whether it's treacherous to discuss matters with the skip manager assuming the workplace culture lets you debate with the higher levels, however the lesson was strikingly clearer. If you do, you commit 'treachery' in the eyes of your reporting manager who themselves may be insecure. This happens more often when the intentions and reasons for someone to approach the skip manager are not made clear to the immediate manager. In the course of time, honest intentions become a perjury, a misrepresentation.

INTERPERSONAL DYNAMICS AND BIASES

In a flat organization, employees have more freedom and elbow-room for decision-making and are empowered to act on their decisions without having to go through a chain of approval. However, what this actually means is that there are fewer (powerful) bosses who control comparatively larger groups of employees as opposed to multiple managers with smaller teams. The interpersonal dynamics in this case are very different. The employee wants more control over daily decisions while the boss has to deal with decisions gone wrong. What makes this more complex is the company culture. If the culture encourages failure, innovation and growth, it is a win-win for both the employee and the manager. If not, the employee thinks they are the manager and the manager is left defenceless as they get penalized for being controlling and 'non-collaborative'. So, in such volatile situations, how do employees judge their leaders at multiple levels? Recency bias, or the phenomenon of a person most easily remembering something that has happened recently, compared to remembering something that may have occurred a while back, plays a big role here for building trust and effective motivation. If you do an employee engagement activity just before the global employee survey, you may get a favourable score. However, if you reprimand them on an ongoing project that is not producing expected results, this will be seen as an 'attack' rather than a 'feedback'. Based on his experiences, Vijaya guarantees that your employee survey results will go south very quickly. Timing is everything. Be cautious about the timing of activities since various biases can affect the outcome of actions. In typical performance appraisal sessions, while there is recency bias at play, leniency bias happens when one manager appears to be more forgiving and accommodating than the others. So, there is a spectrum of managers where some are strict, and others are lenient, and a lot of this behaviour depends on how these managers were treated by their own managers.

As per Vijaya, other than the personal biases, trust is another important aspect of rapport between employees at various levels and its impact on employee survey results. If managers react with trying to pamper your employees after the survey results, they can see through it and will quickly lose trust with them. Leaders who aspire to be well liked by their employees but don't want to take the pains of motivating them, fall into this trap. Vijaya knows he was one of those who like to lead but forget to motivate the teams. Several years ago, Vijay adopted the same, doomed to fail strategy with his own employees and learnt his lesson the hard way. Thankfully Vijaya managed to recover from the blunder that was pointed out to him by his manager and he learnt his lesson. Thankfully he managed to recover when his blunder was pointed out to me by his manager, lesson learnt. It is always more important to be trusted than to be liked. If you are a manager and have not-so-good things to say about your boss, keep your lips tightly closed in the skip-level meeting with him. If you have good things to say, sing away to glory. Skip-level meetings are supposed to be a platform to provide genuine feedback about your manager in terms of what's working and what's not working. But, in reality, these meetings are an avenue to tout your manager's capabilities and earn brownie (loyalty) points that can enhance your chances of a promotion.

Vijaya had a colleague in one of his jobs. In a skip-level meeting, this colleague gave bad feedback about his manager to the director. He said that the manager was not clear with his expectations on project deliverables.

He was providing basic guidance but expected stellar results. The colleague wasn't able to deliver as he was looking for proper written instructions in black and white in order to understand the expectations and he also gave his skip-level feedback in 'black-and white'. The result was that this colleague was asked to go through a 360-degree assessment by his manager even though he was a top performer. Based on the manager's assessment, he got the feedback that he needs to be a good listener and was put under a three-month observation period to monitor the improvement in his listening skills. The colleague was shocked. All was well at the end of the three months, but he learnt his lesson—It's better to keep mum rather than quacking about your boss in skip-level meetings.

In highly people-centric organizations, skip-level feedback is taken seriously. The manager who gets a negative feedback has to actually work on and show improvement on the points raised against him. The progress is ascertained by an improvement in the employee scores during the next feedback cycle. If anyone observes a breach with regard to company policies, it is prudent to document it every time a breach happens. Don't be fooled by the people-centric culture of the company; you need to have a good insurance policy to defend your achievements and stand by your work in case relationships with manager/s go south.

Talking about leadership styles for encouraging communication and transparency at the workplace, Vijaya enumerates that a laissez-faire leader creates a free-for-all culture in the team. Such leaders don't care about the approach, they only want results. Backstabbing and politics will be rife in such an environment. Transactional leaders are micro-managers, they bother you to no end—be ahead of the game by anticipating their needs and over-feed them with information. Strategic guys don't want to be disturbed at all except when you have a visionary idea. Steer clear of these managers; however, when you do meet them, you either make a huge impact or learn from their wisdom and get impacted by their strategic thinking. If you happen to be in their path, make sure you are perceived as extremely flexible and adaptable to change; it implies the ability to pivot priorities which is a way of demonstrating multitasking abilities. If you are like structure, stay away from such managers.

Vijaya's experiences point towards the importance of cultivating psychological safety, encouraging questions and openness in the organization, especially as teams grow and become *diverse with time*.

EMBRACING VULNERABILITIES

Managers must be open minded to acknowledge there are some tasks or situations that may not make the team members feel engaged or comfortable. In such conditions, the team members may not voice out concerns and/or share new thoughts. By understanding the way to build trust withing teams, managers can proactively address the issues that trigger fear in the employees and can pave the way for a more trust-oriented and collaborative work environment. Managers must establish forums where teams can feel comfortable to talk about difficult situations, without worrying about any consequences.

Managers must put technology to use for anonymous and genuine employee feedback. It is a good strategy that can help managers understand where the team stands in level of engagement and passion for their work and workplace. The data collected from the employee feedback can be quickly analysed to get valuable insights. However, most team members believe that employee feedback is only an annual formality, which will not lead to any action taken by the company. Hence, managers should take the initiative to organize regular pulse checks that can reveal the reasons, if any, for cracks in engagement for the employees. It can help the managers pinpoint pain-issues and develop an action plan for improvement.

Establishing a culture of trust between the teams and various managerial levels stems from the ability to practice mutual respect by not always blaming others for things going wrong but also introspecting about one's own actions. It is a common understanding that people working with each other have a need for social acceptance and inclusion as much as respect for their competence and validation of their abilities. The managers and subordinates should be able to ask and give open feedback in a non-defensive manner, enabling positive reinforcement to reaffirm what is going well and take preventive measures to avoid any future negative impact, which can be overcome by transparent feedback. A model of openness is important across all tiers of the organization in order to build trustworthy relationships at the workplace.

The next element to demonstrate authenticity, vulnerability and credibility at the workplace is to embrace conflict. Every difference of opinion does not have to carry a negative undertone. Any conflict between teams and managers must be accepted as a part of the way things are conducted between peers. By embracing conflict, the leaders and managers get a chance to deepen their understanding of people, express empathy and figure out necessary interventions by actively listening to them. This approach leads to an acceptable and executable win-win outcome.

Reinforcing positive behaviours highlights achievements more than failures by avoiding premature blaming and criticism. Often managers are not able to view problematic behaviours objectively. They tend to focus more on the drama in the situation rather than the facts and issues that need solutions. Not too long ago, managers used to ask employees to leave their personal problems at home. However, today in the age of the millennials, the managers encourage the teams to share personal challenges and also help them figure out ways to combat them. Today, managers are quite receptive and want their executives to share aspects of their personal lives, if that can make them more effective at work. Imagine a situation where a manager is having a team meeting and the details of the data to be discussed have been shared beforehand. If the data shows the business of the manager's division is declining, he and the team are quite vulnerable. So rather than defending the reasons for the business to have declined and pulling away a motivated team, it's better for the managers to accept being vulnerable, expose their weakness and share the challenge to recover the business and in-turn the team's reputation. Being vulnerable in the workplace can lead to more trust, transparency and respect.

VALUING SETBACKS AND CELEBRATING RISKS

There are two distinct sets of work environments that one can consider when looking at team management and vulnerabilities. Early stage start-ups act as hubs of innovation; such start-ups maybe ventures by new-age founders or outposts of established companies who would like to keep their innovative and agile minds at work elsewhere as a team. Anyone who deals with such start-ups knows that their description of success is embodied in the learning from failures. In the start-up ecosystem, managers openly tell their teams that failing and restarting is a badge of honour and not something to be worried about. In the early stages of a venture with 10–20 employees, the success is hugely dependent on a series of hypotheses, failures, experiments and perseverance till the desired outcome is achieved. This required time, money and considerable efforts like any other company, but these early-stage innovators don't get bogged down by failures, in fact, they value the setbacks, which help them start anew.

Where early stage ventures are value setbacks, the established organizations lie at the other end of this spectrum. Since these companies have moved ahead of the curve of discovery and experimentation, their focus is execution oriented and delivery of results. Hence, the focus on innovation isn't at the forefront. As such, the managers, subtly, send messages to the employees that failures are unacceptable since they can harm the organization's revenue and/or reputation. In such large organizations, even if managers and the core executives toot the horn of 'failure is okay', they don't mean it most of the times. In the ventures with smaller teams, mistakes are taken in stride, however, as the organizations grow, one can't afford to make the same mistake twice.

The real challenge for managers is to understand whether failures occur when the teams are in ideation mode or execution mode so as to identify where they have leverage and which mistakes come with zero tolerance. If these distinctions are made clearly then the teams also align to them, psychologically. The managers monitor team's performance as per the organization's standard operative procedures that need to be followed with least deviation.

By creating a culture that celebrates risks, managers can give a sense to employees that failure, within acceptable limits and as an exception, is alright, it establishes good culture. Managers must be vulnerable in order for teams to feel like they can do the same. As managers, discussing a failure should always be in a non-threatening way so that team managers can continue thinking out of the box in order to overcome team members can continue higher the obstacles on the way.

Building a culture of psychological safety requires the managers to understand whether their teams fear the work environment or feel empowered by it. When the skip managers lay the groundwork for psychological safety, it drives engagement across verticals.

SHARING PERSONAL INFORMATION

In today's VUCA (volatility, uncertainty, complexity and ambiguity) led world, the personal and professional lives cannot be treated separately. Hence, there are clear lines to be drawn between sharing relevant information and oversharing. When people are under personal stress, it will impact their performance at work and vice versa. Managers often are conflicted whether they should share events in their personal lives with any team member or their superiors, in case it is affecting their work. For example, if the manager is going through a divorce, it can lead to lack of concentration at work. At such a time, the team must know to step up. There may be team members undergoing feelings of insecurity and depression and may not be able to decide whether to tell the manager or not.

Up until a few decades ago, managers and teams hesitated to share personal information with one another, but things have changed in that regard nowadays. Sharing personal challenges across different hierarchical levels has become much more acceptable now. Today, employees feel a sense of support by being honest about their personal lives with colleagues and managers. However, if not balanced well, sharing can lead to uncomfortable situations at the workplace.

A person might end up oversharing or miscommunicating by revealing too much about their personal challenges to the wrong person. This can alienate people who feel uncomfortable with the amount of personal information one shares. Alternately, recounting personal issues to colleagues and managers who don't have your best interests at heart can lead them to take advantage of your vulnerable situation. On the other hand, continuous reference to personal issues in front of colleagues and managers can lead them to believe you can't deliver your best. This can push you down the ladder at the time of assignment of good projects and opportunities.

The difference between relevant information and oversharing is the intention of the person sharing the information. If the organization is passing through a tough business phase and needs to retrench people, sharing unsubstantiated information can question the credibility of the person. Below are a few examples of situations where it becomes necessary to differentiate between genuine issues and blemished information.

- **Sympathy sharing.** Many times, employees go to skip managers and share personal matters to gain sympathy as a means to conceal mistakes. Best practices and root cause analysis of issues should be shared at all levels so that the attempt is considered credible and authentic. However, oversharing may sometimes be for the purpose of gaining the manager's pity so as to divert attention from a gaffe or blunder made by the employee. If employees, at whichever hierarchical level, succeed in gaining sympathy by such means, it becomes a pattern for them to invent new problems or magnify small issues, till someone cottons on to their schemes.

- **Building relationships.** Employees want the senior management to notice them and their good work for better mobility in the workplace. The best way to achieve a manager's/ boss's trust and appreciation is through skilled performance at work and pleasant behaviour. However, some employees choose to take short-cuts to develop good relations with the seniors by oversharing personal information in an attempt to gain a sense of intimacy and hoping it builds trust eventually.

- **Sharing anxiety.** Employees who are unable to handle anxiety effectively have a tendency to blame their surroundings for such anxiety and want to share these issues with their colleagues very frequently. Such employees have a habit of revealing pain points at all times, a behaviour which amplifies when they are in front of the senior management.

Once there is a good rapport between an employee and the manager, there are certain situations when an exchange of personal information is acceptable. However, both sides should be comfortable with such sharing. Do people share their health issues with peers and superiors, which may impact their performance in the short term, to be transparent or to just let it off their minds?

There can be situations where the management wants a manager to relocate overseas for few months to oversee a critical project and the person may not be able to go due to personal reasons. In such situations, if the person knows his personal constraints, he should inform the management about his inability to travel even before he is asked to. Between teams and managers, the legitimacy of personal information depends on the nature and timing of information shared.

TRUST AND EFFECTIVE MOTIVATION

An experience of Shankar Mallapur, a senior professional at a global technology giant, a Stanford LEAD alumnus and more recently, a life and career coach.

What we Think We Become.

—*Buddha*

It was early 2009. The world was still recovering from the gaping wounds left behind by the financial crisis in 2008. Shankar was working with a large global technology consulting company. The company had operations in over 50 countries, divided into three geographic zones: America, Europe and growth markets. Their organization was aligned by industry verticals, with deep specialization in each industry including financial services, health, communications and consumer goods.

The company had managed to overcome the financial crisis relatively well, though it had shed a few employees. The company was regarded as a leader in technology services and had a progressive, futuristic outlook. It was eagerly waiting for growth to pick up in its clients' industries.

Dan and Mark were two directors responsible for strategy and growth, Mark for the Europe zone and Dan for the growth markets. Shankar worked as a manager in a delivery project and was a witness to their contrasting approaches for driving growth.

STRATEGY FOR REVIVING GROWTH

Both teams formulated strategies jointly to work with key clients in order to improve growth. Some actions were adapted to suit different geographies and client requirements. The actions included the following:

- Helping clients increase technology adoption through automation,
- Overcoming barriers to change,
- Scenario analysis for managing under uncertainty, and
- Winning over influential buyers.

Both Mark and Dan had differing styles of working. Mark was a traditional old school and experienced manager with a good performance track record. Dan was relatively a newcomer in the organization and his approach was a bit different—he believed in continuous learning and applying new techniques and frameworks in his daily work.

Mark reached out to the leadership teams of Sales and Projects and laid out his plans for helping clients to adopt digital transformation and winning over influential buyers. A broad consensus on the plan was reached; the emphasis was on execution.

Dan tried a different approach. He was of the opinion that beliefs determine thoughts, which influence our behaviour and actions, which in turn impacts the results. He felt that a person's belief system can act like a magnet, which attracts what they think about, with consistency in performance and empathetic handling of people at the workplace. A person's thoughts that may be driven by fear, worry, anger, positivity or any other emotion will become their reality. He gave an analogy for this: A person's thoughts are like a hammer, a very effective tool in the right hands and very dangerous in the wrong hands. According to him, this includes the habit of oversharing personal information to gain leverage against others. Often, in challenging times, people think more about what they do not want and what they fear rather than what they do want—their dreams, goals and desires. This is one of the main reasons, he said, that people have to struggle to achieve the outcomes they want in life.

It follows the law of attraction and the ability to control one's thoughts. He coached the teams on the fact that words, thoughts and actions of achievers radiate confidence and trained them on concentrating on areas they had control over, rather than those that they could not control. His motto was 'this phase too shall pass'. According to him, when people worry about things happening in the world over which they have no control, it saps their strength. Excessive worry, which is a form of fear, needs to be vanquished.

Our brains exhibit neuroplasticity and can be rewired. By modifying our thoughts to be more positive, we can strengthen areas that stimulate positive feeling and rewire our brain. Dan felt everyone can lead more fulfilled professional lives by following these principles.

STRATEGY FOR EFFECTIVE MOTIVATION AND TRUST BUILDING

Think positive. Based on how you perceive the world, your inner dialogues guide your daily actions and decisions.

Reframe. Replace worrisome thoughts with positive ones. Transform your thoughts from 'I am weak' to 'I am strong'.

Avoid self-defeatist language. Try to avoid worlds like 'perhaps' and 'hopefully' to 'yes, I can do it'.

Start and end communications on a positive note. End with 'cheers', or even a smiley in informal emails.

Start and end the day on a positive note. Start the day with a smile and the feeling that 'I will make it a successful one'. End the day with noting your accomplishments.

Dan's thinking was unconventional for a corporate setting. While everybody did not buy into his thinking, his drive and personality ensured that everyone agreed to give it their best shot. He believed that it is not external events that matter, but how we respond to them, in our individual capacities, which determines the results. We always have a choice and how we respond in a situation is entirely up to us.

Dan's team consistently trained and supported their Sales and Service Delivery Project teams with the new training. The team constantly motivated everyone with their constructive and much needed positive-message posters, displayed all around the office as well as regular emails. He thus helped the teams make fundamental changes in their habits, to make them success oriented.

OUTCOMES

Mark's team was able to increase the sales for their geography by over 18 per cent over the next year. This was well beyond past results. It came off a lower base of performance numbers in the preceding year.

Dan's team was able to increase their sales by over 37 per cent. These changes impacted not just the team members' sales for the following year but impacted many aspects of their lives like practicing patience with critical thinking.

The change in their beliefs influenced their habits, resulting in improved decision-making and far-reaching actions. The clear lesson was that they needed to adopt unconventional strategies to achieve extraordinary results.

DEVELOPMENT V/S REDUCTIVE SUPERVISORS

Managers and their teams feel strongly motivated when they are made to realize the potential in them. If the skip managers take the first step to motivate the subordinate managers and teams to realize their capabilities to drive desired outcomes, they remain self-motivated for a long time. Building trust and effective motivation also depends on the supervisory styles of the immediate bosses and skip managers. The 'developmental' supervisors stimulate motivation and 'reductive' supervisors inhibit motivation. Developmental managers assume the principal role in problem-solving rather than dictating mandates. These types of managers provide the right direction and information for teams to enhance performance. Reductive managers have a propensity to quash motivation, inhibit positive expressions and can induce symptoms of forced acceptance and self-protective behaviours among their employees. This leads to unattractive goal setting, red-tapeism and interpersonal conflicts. In order to be developmental in building trust and motivation, the managers have to demonstrate self-realization and enthusiasm to embrace creativity of the team members. The developmental managers develop subordinates to be competitive. The developmental behaviour does not surface automatically and intuitively in managers; it needs intellectual understanding, self-confidence and ability to make things right in case the teams falter. This is further enhanced by interpersonal competence and existence of a helpful multi-level management system.

FURTHER READINGS

'Creating Psychological Safety at Work.' [Podcast] https://hbr.org/podcast/2019/01/creating-psychological-safety-in-the-workplace

Forkman, Zenger. 2018. 'Research Shows the Best Way to Motivate.' https://zengerfolkman.com/articles/research-shows-the-best-way-to-motivate-others/

Giacoman, Augusto. 2017. 'The Strength of Vulnerable Leaders.' https://www.strategy-business.com/blog/The-Strength-of-Vulnerable-Leaders?gko=74926

BECOMING A BETTER MANAGER

We know that corporate warzones have borrowed a lot from the structures in the defence forces. Most of the companies have a vertical hierarchical structure rather than a horizontal set up like a sports team or an orchestra playing in true sync and harmony. It is due to the rigid horizontal structuring that the organizations tend to be led more by processes than people as the team size grows.

However, Zenger Folkman's research revealed that managers who ask and listen are rated as better and more effective managers than the ones who spend most of their time ordering their employees around. Most people tend to picture managers as people who talk more and hear less, however, Folkman's research also found out that as one progresses up the ranks, the preference changes to 'ask and learn'.

Being a manager should never be considered as an opportunity to have a right to shout and talk excessively. One should never view being a manager as a license to increase the volume and keep taking. A lot of successful managers have demonstrated that rather than being domineering, surrendering to the new ideas of a younger team sometimes brings out better results.

In this digital age people have all the opportunities to pick other peoples' brains and learn. However, in the era of chat messengers and instant communication, managers do not see the difference between appropriate hours and odd hours for communication. Hence, they write to others whenever convenient to oneself than others. If a manager is not able to ask and learn, it could lead to the team derailing.

HOW TO BE A 'BETTER MANAGER'

Managers who ask and learn from team members, even those who are multiple levels below them, can make more informed decisions. Most managers are natural speakers, however, the crafts they need to develop, and master, is listening and asking. That's what makes a better skip manager. A skip manager who is able to master the art of asking becomes more like a team's coach. Their objective is not to dethrone the team manager but to help the team members challenge the status quo and give them the liberty to think freely and out of the box. I have witnessed conversations with skip managers that were 'questions only' and statements were phrased as questions rather than prescriptions. That also helped the skip managers to maintain a neutral image and not appear biased. Skip managers don't undergo training on how to change their behaviours to be more questioning oriented. However, there are few ways it can be done. Being a listener reduces the 'big personality intimidating' effect and the teams can approach the skips more easily with genuine needs. Consider applying the OCEAN theory, also referred to as the Big Five Model of Personality, to traits of managers: It is also referred to as the OCEAN Theory: Openness to experience, Conscientiousness, Extroversion, Agreeableness and Neuroticism.

OPENNESS TO EXPERIENCE

Openness to experience is referred to as a manager's span and scope of risk-taking, initiative and imagination. The managers demonstrating this trait have a desire to try new ways of addressing problems and appreciate out of the box thinkers. The managers who score high on this parameter are creative and curious. As such, they need teams that can change their work priorities and projects at a short notice, since these managers don't prefer to stay within the comfort zone and act conventionally. It seems companies like Qualcomm, Apple, Intel have such managers. This is assumed since these companies don't sell products to the end consumer directly, however, they keep exploring new ways of communication and brand recall. Their product roadmaps evolution is futuristic. These companies create markets and take risks associated with it. It cannot be done without progressive, visionary managers and leaders.

CONSCIENTIOUSNESS

Conscientiousness is about reliability and dependability. There are always 'go to managers' in every organization. When there are doubts in decision-making, the people are driven to managers who have demonstrated reliability and dependability over the years. This is based on how the managers' previous decisions fared and benefited the organization. Such managers are welcomed back by their ex-employers in case they would like to work together again. These managers are goal-oriented, organized and are never impulsive.

EXTROVERSION

Extrovert managers are those who like to dominate conversations and are very active socially. They believe in the width of a network more than its depth. Self-assured and proud, such managers are assertive, socially confident and prefer jobs that require interacting with people. These managers are more about action and much less about introspection.

AGREEABLENESS

Ever seen managers who seem sympathetic and affectionate most of the time at office? These are the ones who can get along easily with people. These managers are never blunt or sarcastic.

It's difficult to fathom whether such managers are agreeable on the surface and become assertive later on, or they actually like to score high on being well liked.

NEUROTICISM

Neuroticism is the OCEAN trait which is a measure of emotional stability. Most managers are either aggressive or defensive. However, the most successful managers are usually ones who can control their emotions and not be overcome by sadness, anxiety or frustration. The lesser the neuroticism the better, such managers are more confident and adventurous. In tough situations they can see the light at the end of the tunnel.

As mentioned in the book, *Essentials of Organizational Behavior*, the OCEAN trait that influences the performance of managers the most is conscientiousness. Managers possessing this trait are ideal managers and CXOs with strong leadership aspects. Such managers are very knowledgeable in their fields and believe in life-long learning but don't like to adhere to any structured re-skilling and up-skilling programmes; instead they rely on learning on the job and on a 'need-to-know' basis. The flipside is that such managers may not be able to adapt to the changing cultural situations and put work over everything else.

CREATING BETTER LEADERS

Ruchi Tandon is a Director of SAP SuccessFactors in California. She is passionate about Human Resource Tech and the difference it can make in an organization's success. She derives energy by creating employees' engagement experiences. She shared her very interesting opinion about the kind of managers and leaders who can work well with the Generations X and Z.

Companies should not try to create 'better managers' as we don't need managers but leaders to lead the extremely talented, knowledgeable workforce comprising primarily of Generation X, xennials, millennials and Generation Z, all of whom have very different motivations to come to work every single day.

It is imperative that organizations shift gears and focus on how to create better leaders. Leaders live to practice ways of harnessing the best behaviours and performance from their teams while managers just tend to get the required work done from the teams. Leaders have others following them and managers have people working for them. Having worked for some of the best and the worst managers in her career, Ruchi is an expert who advises organizations on building better, high-performance leaders instead of managers, and this in turn ensures that the workforce thrives, and everyone is motivated to do their best. Some of the steps that organizations can take are discussed below.

ESTABLISH TRUST AND OWNERSHIP

It is very important that organizations entrust and empower their leaders with the task of leading their teams in a way that can drive their teams and bring out the best in each individual. Large organizations cannot have a one-size-fits-all approach, as these organizations have multiple teams and different teams have distinct motivations based on regional, cultural and demographic differences and to build a great workforce, the leadership should acknowledge these differences and trust their line managers to lead their teams keeping these cultural differences in mind.

Ruchi was part of this great team where the global head of function allowed the regional heads to run their teams keeping in mind the cultural and regional nuances so that the teams can be most effective and thrive. When you hire smart people, you need to step back and empower them to do their best.

BUILD A CULTURE OF EXTREME FEEDBACK

To develop great leaders and help them create thriving teams, executive leadership should be open to all kinds of feedback and welcome criticism from everyone. Ruchi had an opportunity to be part of the keynote speech of Adam Grant in which he talked about building a culture of extreme feedback by focusing on how you respond to it. As per Ray Dalio, the billionaire founder of the hedge fund Bridgewater Associates, 'One of the biggest tragedies of mankind is people holding in their opinions in their heads.' If feedback is welcomed and celebrated by the top management, they can build a culture of openness where doing things in the best interest of the company supersedes everything. Candid feedback is shared fearlessly when there is a great deal of trust in management. Netflix is one company that celebrates open/candid feedback especially when it is given to the top management. No wonder it is one of the best companies to work at.

RESULT-ORIENTED PULSE SURVEY

Ruchi has seen large organizations being big on employee engagement by conducting pulse surveys for every single change that is implemented in the organization. However, she observes that there is no point in conducting these surveys if one plans to do nothing about that feedback. If there is no change, people realize that their voice does not really count, and they stop engaging—If companies notice low engagement from employees, they should be cognizant of the fact that this could be the reason for it. Listen and really listen and respect and appreciate freedom of expression. The top management should make sure that the feedback received through pulse surveys is shared with all relevant internal stakeholders like employees, divisional heads and managers, and action items are documented and followed through to drive the necessary changes. As Culture Amp's CEO Didier Elzinga says, 'The most typical reason people don't want to fill out your survey is because they haven't seen any action being taken since the last one. They don't have survey fatigue; they have lack-of-action fatigue.'

PROVIDE UNIQUE OPPORTUNITIES TO THRIVE

A good leader is able to create opportunities for individuals in line with their personal motivations that drive people to give their best. A good leader understands each individual, depending on where are they are in their career, is driven by different factors that are important to them. For instance, for one employee an ability to pursue a course from a prestigious institution might be better and for another USD 15,000 in Restricted Stock Units may serve as a motivation; similarly for some flexible working hours could make all the difference while for another it could be work–life balance that could act as a motivating factor; and some thrive on recognition and appreciation. A leader provides their team with opportunities to fuel their motivations. The leadership should empower the line managers to create these opportunities for allowing their teams to thrive.

FAIRNESS

It makes a huge difference when people have faith that their managers are fair and can be trusted to have their backs. Ruchi had a manager who made such a difference to the team morale and how they worked with each other and with customers by being fair to everyone in the team, and whoever worked with him professionally, believed in him. He worked effortlessly with everyone getting things done, not only his team's work but also helped cross-functional teams with their work if required. He built trust within the team and brought out the best in all the members. Ruchi and the team were able to share every confidential and personal opinion with him.

Ruchi fully believes that the responsibility of building a culture of trust, feedback, integrity and fairness lies with the top leadership. Rewarding behaviours that drive the above values is what will help build non-toxic workplaces and make an organization an exceptional place to work at.

HOW TO CONDUCT PRODUCTIVE MEETINGS

In order to be a better manager and a skip manager, one has to be in control of their behaviour and develop effective questioning techniques so that the employees can give relevant and intelligent responses. Below are a few ideas that may help manager to conduct productive meetings.

READINESS AND DISCIPLINE

Kunal, a skip manager, always found the meetings with the subordinate manager and his team to be largely ineffective. There used to be chaos in the room and lack of meeting objectives. Kunal analysed the situation and realized that the subordinate manager and the team members were always coming to him with last minute preparations. This resulted in a meeting that never had any proper outcome; Kunal figured that the subordinate manager was, maybe, doing this by design. Having come to this conclusion, Kunal started asking for a briefing note or presentation with the meeting objectives to be shared with him two days in advance. The subordinate manager took exception by citing the heavy workload with the team. Kunal decided to be direct and said that if the team cannot be ready for the meeting a day in advance, then the meeting is a mere formality. The manager and team realized that Kunal was quite serious about their preparedness and discipline, and they started sending the brief two days in advance. This gave Kunal time to reply with the topics of interest a day in advance. This helped the team prepare to discuss the topics shared by Kunal and the meetings became more productive as the questions became streamlined to specific topics and helped with the learning curve.

ENHANCING RESPONSES, ENCOURAGING QUESTIONS

A good manager is able to develop and build upon conversations with others and improvise upon responses based on the answers they receive. Sandeep was a senior manager who firmly believed that the meetings with subordinate managers and the team members were to get appraised of the situation on ground. However, he didn't encourage conversations around the issues being faced by the team and preferred an update-only meeting rather than discussing the team's problems. When the subordinate manager, Sunil, pointed out that the team meetings should also have a problem-solving session, Sandeep told him that if the answers, suggestions and resolutions for problems came from Sandeep, then the team members will eventually stop appreciating or looking up to the direct manager. Sunil was heading another team and had a different skip manager to report to. This manager, at the team meetings, wanted him to include problematic areas for discussion and always encouraged his team to talk to him about any work-related issues the team was facing during these meetings. In order to ensure his words or suggestions don't become prescriptive, Sunil asked relevant questions in the skip meetings, guiding the manager to compare the situation at hand with another situation; in terms of how and why they won or lost a particular contract and the reasons for the same. The subordinate manager felt empowered and the team knew that the meetings will always give them a fresh perspective to a problem. Sunil kept a friendly body language in meetings and never failed to build on responses. Before the meeting ended, Sunil ensured he asked everyone around the table if anyone had a question. The people felt respected and involved. Sandeep's meetings became routine, transactional and boring. Sunil's meeting remained outcome oriented and were attended with enthusiasm.

NOTHING SHOULD GO UNNOTICED

There must be an observer in the meetings with the skip manager, who must note down important points and the minutes of the meeting and keep a track of questions that remain unanswered. Roger, a skip manager in an insurance company had to meet his subordinate manager and team every week. This was due to the nature of work and the amount of challenges that needed to be discussed on a regular basis. Roger knew that missing the details on even one case could prove be problematic. Every time a meeting was arranged, Roger nominated one person from the team to keep a record of the minutes of the meeting. It always made the meetings structured and outcome oriented. Since the observer was rotated in every meeting, no one felt like a clerk or an executive assistant. Through this exercise, Roger also discovered that sometimes he focuses more on speaking rather than listening and asking questions. He always made it a point to not repeat this in the next meeting.

NOBODY IS PERFECT

Perfection is a problem with no cure. Many managers tend to compromise on time taken to act because they want everything to be perfect and precise. Rajan was newly hired in an organization as a skip manager. The exiting manager asked him to continue with the fortnightly skip meetings. Rajan appreciated the feedback to keep up with the best practices but was not sure if he should get involved in regular discussions with the subordinate managers and their teams too soon. Leading and holding conversations didn't come naturally to Rajan; however, he realized the importance of the meetings and didn't want to stop the practice. He decided to continue the meetings but made them informal by convening the meetings in cafes rather than the office so that heading such meetings can become an 'acquired taste'. He informed the team that for rapport building the fortnightly meetings will be held at a café for the next two months. Then he ensured that the sessions started with random subjects like sports or celebrity gossip. The subordinate managers and teams appreciated and understood that Rajan was not an 'aim and fire guy' and they went with the flow. They also looked at Rajan as being like any other human, none of whom are perfect. At his end, Rajan knew he needed practice to overcome the fear of immediate conversations and to learn to ask the right questions.

WHAT SETS A MANAGER APART

Of the many traits of successful managers, three stand out. These are seldom paid attention to and get lost in the day-to-day struggle for existence.

STANDING UP FOR YOUR TEAM

Ash was the regional head of a division and five managers reported to him. One of those managers, Jan, came from a public sector enterprise. Ash had no respect for the guy. During meetings with the country manager, Ash had a tendency to put down Jan and the others could see it too. Every other manager joked about what would happen to Jan in the monthly review meetings. Ash gave five government enterprise clients to Jan, knowing those accounts were almost dead. Jan had a team of three people and he focused on his work. Four months later Ash was facing a business challenge when two of their clients that contributed to 40 per cent of the business were poached by competition. Ash was nervous and called for ad hoc meetings and lost his cool in the meeting with his team. Two days later Jan walked into Ash's room and handed him the contracts of the company with two new government enterprise clients. Ash looked at the papers casually and eventually realized that these new contracts would cover up almost 20 per cent of the loss expected to be incurred by the exit of the two corporate clients. Ash thanked him and asked Jan if he could do anything for him. Jan asked him to stand up for him and have his back. He also promised to have Ash's back. After six months Ash's region clocked the highest number of sales from the government enterprise business. From this incident, he realized that the team expects managers to support them and have their back; it keeps them motivated and work harder.

CAREER PLANNING

Amara had been working at the same company for ten years and was currently a director. The next promotion would make her a Vice President. Amara had handled three assignments in the 10 years, with different teams and roles. In her current assignment, Amara was handling P&L for a business that was 40 per cent ahead in revenues. She was very good at managing her department, still no one from her previous teams ever wanted to work with her again. HR had noted this trend and instituted a feedback session with her ex-teammates. Everyone appreciated her work and managerial abilities but didn't want to work with her again. On probing they said that Amara doesn't plan her own career very well, so they get stuck at levels below her. Had she aspired to plan her career moves better we could have also got better opportunities. HR realized that people working under Amara never got a job rotation and were seldom promoted, though they had handsome salary hikes based on performance. At her end, Amara had made up her mind to begin and end her career at the same organization. It seemed that she would be in the same place, working at her own pace for the next 20–35 years; people working under her would also not be able get new opportunities, and their career will also end up having a ceiling. The HR team ensured they created a 5-year career plan with Amara according to which she would get a mix of new and old employees. That also ensured that the deserving team members got job rotations and sometimes got promoted to lead smaller divisions, with Amara's strong recommendation. Amara realized that if a manager doesn't plan his/her career better, their teams also suffer.

INTERACT AS HUMANS

Barry landed in a chemicals company with offices in 13 countries. He had six direct reportees of which two were 10 years elder to him. As a manager, it was the first time Barry was going to manage people more experienced and aged than him. For some reason he developed a preconceived defensive strategy and thought that these two veterans will cause a nuisance. Making an assumption without intent was Barry's first mistake as a manager. As a manager, one must learn to deal and communicate with people of different ages, gender, religious beliefs and backgrounds. One should never doubt their worth and presume that others are enemies. Barry started putting down his guard and figured out a way to earn their respect by listening to them and respecting their age, however, ensuring that the assessment of their work was on merit. In this way, the team worked on just fine.

EFFECTIVE SKIP MANAGERS' MEETINGS

Managers must do what it takes to create realistic objectives during the meetings. That way, within less time more outcomes can be achieved. Skip management can be tricky and there is no easy route to fulfil one's responsibilities. Skip-level meetings can truly impact employees at all levels and also help avoid the creation of 'biggest personality' perceptions, because of which managers appear like out-of-reach bosses. Productivity and work done in organization depends a lot on skip-management meetings.

The skip managers hold team meetings to get answers to the questions listed below.

- How are the managers really doing and enhancing team productivity?
- What's really happening at the ground level?
- Is the skip manager missing anything important?

Being a multiplier manager, the skips have to develop leaders under them and keep a close eye on the macro behaviours across the division. They must know what's at stake. These meetings are about getting a sense of the health of the division. If there is a bad subordinate manager and the skip is not able to identify him/her, chances are that the division can lose high performers and once that happens, it may be too late to salvage the situation. People who leave organizations due to their managers usually find other avenues to make themselves heard. When they realize that the levels above are inaccessible, they find a new job and leave. If the skip manager is able to develop a rapport with people across the division, attrition can be avoided.

Further, a good rapport between the employees is also important for skip-level meetings because the initial one or two gatherings are awkward for everyone. Normally there is silence interspersed with awkward coughs and clutter of coffee cups. As such, skip managers prefer a brief introduction of the team members from the subordinate managers to avoid putting anyone in an awkward situation. Imagine a situation when during a skip-level meeting, people start planning for an office party. One person in the team stays silent, shies away from the conversation and is almost in tears. No one is bothered that he/she just suffered the loss of a dear one and party planning at such a time can be upsetting. Had the skip manager known about the person's tragedy, he/she could have been spared the grief. Hence, the first few skip-level meetings should have an agenda that everyone can appreciate.

If no one is aware where to begin, open-ended questions addressed at all attendees are the best way to break the ice and start conversations. Discussing a hobby or asking why someone chose to join the organization are successful, non-threatening icebreakers. However, sometimes similar questions create awkward moments. For instance, a question by the skip manager about everyone's colleges can be a matter of pride for the people who attended top-tier colleges, but it can be disheartening and awkward for people who attended private or unheard-of colleges. Such questions that can create a divide between the team should be avoided, instead generic topics should be asked.

Proper skip-level meetings are able to bring about and nail down issues before they become very big. Catching and fixing problems when they are small is much more cost effective than if they boil over and need the expertise of higher-level executives.

PARALLEL V/S PYRAMID SYSTEM

Marta Ferrer Garcia lives in Madrid. She is a Stanford LEAD alumnus with six years of corporate experience. She is an authority on how effective managerial leadership impacts the career professionals at her level.

There are managers who command and managers who lead; the difference in outcomes lies in the virtue of the second type of managers who actively listen to their employees' ideas and troubles and make them feel valued and appreciated. Having a work environment with committed employees, who feel their voices are considered, and who feel driven by a common purpose, is the cornerstone of successful organizations.

Is there a bubble around the idea of leadership? Leadership is a word that was propelled in the early 2000s and now is used too often in various contexts. Everyone wanted to be a leader, wants their company culture based on leadership and no one seems to like working in a company that lacks effective leadership. Enterprises are undergoing a transformation, and this is reflected or even caused by the evolution of the workforce and its management chain.

Nowadays, it is more common to see organizations working with a parallel system rather than a pyramidal one. Let's explore the differences between the two systems. Parallel systems allow to situate all employees at the same level, alongside managers and directors, based on a liquid system in which the information flows equally to everyone. This type of system is commonly seen in small to medium enterprises and start-ups; they enable employees to feel they are a key part of the team and have unforbidden access to managers and seniors. The CXOs can have a clear understanding and awareness of the team's performance due to transparency in communication. This leads to easy information access at all levels that otherwise could have been delayed in a bureaucratic organizational structure.

Bigger enterprises commonly function as a pyramidal system, which sets a clear chain of command, the company is structured as a ladder, and typically each level reports to the one above and supervises the one below. The problem with this system is if one of these levels fail, the communication flow is altered in both directions.

Both systems have their own benefits and disadvantages. The application of each system should be aligned with the company's mission and growth; however, it is to be noted that both systems need a good set of leaders to make the company grow and achieve its mission.

A leader is at the frontline guiding its team and helping them develop and work to their full potential. If the leader is not considered a part of the team, then they are not setting the right direction or path for the team to pursue. In such situations the team members will have much more difficulty collaborating for the greater good of higher performance to meet goals and objectives.

The African proverb, 'If you want to go fast, go alone. If you want to go far, go together', provides the difference between good leadership and 'each man for his own' leadership. Some leaders improve the team culture and the communication between team members, which is essential for the future of the company. Managers need to know their team well, what drives them as individuals and what makes them a unique team when their strengths are combined. If a leader doesn't not know the strengths of his/her team, it's difficult to leverage them; this eventually leads to a performance lacking in results. Leaders, being at the frontline guide their teams, but they might also end up misleading their vision. If a captain only looks at the ship's prow and never turns back, he will not know what is happening at the boat's stern end. Leaders must speak to communicate the big picture and the tasks for the teams to perform; however, they also need to hear from the teams about their views and versions of the work in hand. No one has a 360-degree view; managers can only look in one direction at a time, they need the team to be their eyes in the opposite direction.

A great leader surrounds himself/herself with great experts not always because they can't do well in that area, but because they know they need to focus on leading the team, as such, they can't micro manage and may not be able to pick up on the little but essential things; this is where a team comes into the picture. If, when a crisis arises, leaders give orders without consulting the vision their team can provide, they lack being aware of half of the possibilities. Although they are indeed guiding their team towards a resolution, they are not leading but directing them without letting them be part of the decision.

This kind of leadership breaks the trust in the leadership, running the risk of having them think that their opinions are not worth a consideration, which could decrease employee engagement with the common purpose of the organization.

This does not mean that leaders should always prioritize their team's perspective above their own. A leader should actively listen to his/her team's opinions and then choose the best solution even if it does not align with his/her team's preference. They should explain their decisions and by doing so, they would show appreciation for the team.

Even in the workforce, leaders are persons that we decide to follow because we want to, and not because we are forced to. Admittedly, if you want to get paid for your work, you do need to follow them, but this does not change the idea that leaders are still created by the vision that their teams have of them, and not the position they hold in the management chain.

THE CLOSURE

When skip-level meetings are wound up, they should end with clear actionable steps. More importantly, the steps to be taken should be owned by the subordinate managers and the team. Potential outcomes of a skip-level meeting may include the following.

IMMEDIATE STEPS

- Send the information requested by the skip manager or offered by the team to give the skip manager more insights into the discussion.

- Create a plan to execute the decisions taken in the meeting and outline points that need to be discussed again with the skip manager (the subordinate manager needs to be in charge of this).

- Act on the advice of the skip manager. However, the onus of figuring out the means of acting on the advice and delivering outcomes is on the subordinate manager and the team.

CONFIDENCE BUILDING

While concluding a meeting, the skip manager must make his/her stand on the matter under discussion and his willingness to back the teams, clear. Even though the discussion might have been about fixing issues, sharing updates or implementation of a new idea, the skip manager must end the meeting on a motivational note.

POST MEETING DISCUSSION

Once the meeting comes to an end, the skip manager must re-discuss the pertinent issues again with the persons assigned to the tasks along with the subordinate manager. They may want to align priorities in a different way. The skip manager should keep a track of the final call taken by his/her team on a particular issue and let the team own the process and outcomes. The skip manager should ensure that the employees at different levels know that their concerns will be addressed but the skip bandwidth needs to be used for addressing critical strategic needs along with operational and transactional needs.

Skip-level meetings are a very impactful and rewarding investment in the success of an organization. With the skip managers' support, many a times daunting tasks look easier and the impossible becomes achievable.

With a little planning, preparation and compassion, the skip managers can get the best out of their teams and provide the middle managers with the necessary boost to stay on their toes. Ultimately better managers retain the right people, generate loyalty and create a brigade of achievers.

To conclude, I am reproducing a note from my earlier career as a corporate professional, which will provide a glimpse into the role of my manager in ensuring my success.

My first award for excellence in career was in the year 1999 from Lucent Technologies.

Moving from a customer support to sales role, this award came as a positive endorsement and reinforcement of my decision. No two ways about the fact that my manager had a big role to play in making me achieve the award.

As an effective manager, he was able to figure out what's unique about each of his employees and he used that to elevate our performance. My manager encouraged skip-level meetings so that I could gain a diversified perspective of the work to be done.

Managers are either like checkers or like chess. In checkers, the pieces are uniform and interchangeable. In chess, each piece moves uniquely, and one needs to know how each piece moves to make a full play.

Great managers understand the abilities of each person and then pack a punch for a coordinated win. Out of the whole team in India, four of us were chosen for the coveted recognition.

The award ceremony was in Bangkok where we met Lucent Technology's global leadership. The experience was beyond words.

The manager watched from a distance; he had played his part. The team was what he had envisioned for us: a bunch of crazy achievers.

FURTHER READINGS

'Lead Your Team with the Big Five Model.' 2019. https://www.michiganstateuniversityonline.com/resources/leadership/lead-your-team-with-big-five-model/

Robbins, Stephen P., and Timothy A. Judge. 2018. *Essentials of Organizational Behavior*, Fourteenth Edition. Edinburg: Pearson.

ABOUT THE AUTHOR

Rishi is a 48-years-old Stanford LEAD alumnus with dual masters in management and an engineering degree, and with 27+ years of experience. He has authored three books, published in the last five years.

Rishi is the former CXO of Fortune 500 companies and transitioned into being a start-up scale up specialist, career management coach and an academician. His coaching beneficiaries include super-senior and middle management leadership teams of corporates, entrepreneurial ventures and students at academic institutions.

From 1993 to 2014, for over two decades, Rishi held strategic and operational roles in Sony, Qualcomm, Ericsson, BP/Castrol, Avaya and HCL. Having received several awards and accolades for his professionalism and speed of execution, his last corporate assignment was as the interim MD and VP of Sony Mobile Communications. Rishi has co-authored research papers with laureates of Oxford University and IIT Kharagpur and is passionate about impactful outcomes and lifelong learning.